BERING SEA

DEADLIEST CATCH™

Deadliest Catch: Desperate Hours
Writer: Dan Weeks
Contributing Designer: Diana Van Winkle
Copy Chief: Terri Fredrickson
Copy Editor: Kevin Cox
Publishing Operations Manager:
 Karen Schirm
Senior Editor, Asset and Information
Manager: Phillip Morgan
Edit and Design
Production Coordinator: Mary Lee Gavin
Art and Editorial Sourcing Coordinator:
 Jackie Swartz
Book Production Managers: Pam Kvitne,
 Marjorie J. Schenkelberg, Mark Weaver
Imaging Center Operator: Richard Van Winkle
Contributing Photographer: Dan Weeks
Contributing Copy Editor: Ira Lacher
Contributing Proofreaders: Stan West,
 Mike Maine, Jody Speer, David Krause

Meredith® Books
Editor in Chief: Gregory H. Kayko
Executive Director, Design: Matt Strelecki
Managing Editor: Amy Tincher-Durik
Editor at Large/Group Manager:
 Larry Erickson
Senior Associate Design Director:
 Chad Jewell
Marketing Product Manager:
 Mark Mooberry
Executive Director, Marketing and
New Business:
 Kevin Kacere
Director, Marketing and Publicity:
 Amy Nichols
Executive Director, Sales: Ken Zagor
Director, Operations: George A. Susral
Director, Production: Douglas M. Johnston
Business Director: Janice Croat

Senior Vice President: Karla Jeffries
Vice President and General Manager:
 Douglas J. Guendel

Meredith Publishing Group
President: Jack Griffin
Executive Vice President: Doug Olson

Meredith Corporation
Chairman of the Board: William T. Kerr
President and Chief Executive Officer:
Stephen M. Lacy

In Memoriam: E.T. Meredith III
(1933–2003)

Discovery Channel
Book Development Team
President & General Manager,
 Discovery Channel: John Ford
Vice-President, Licensing: Carol LeBlanc
Director, Licensing: Brigid Ferraro
Manager, Licensing: Caitlin Erb
Designer: Bridget Stoyko

All of us at Meredith Books are dedicated
to providing you with information and
ideas to enhance your life. We welcome
your comments and suggestions. Write
to us at: Meredith Books, New Business
Development Department, 1716 Locust St.,
Des Moines, IA 50309-3023.

Bering Sea chart artwork courtesy of
OceanGrafix, St. Paul, Minnesota

Table of Contents

No dollies and grips here! *Deadliest Catch* photographers had to rely on their own ingenuity and the equipment at hand when shooting at sea.

An epic journey begins

Foreword by Thom Beers,
Creator and Executive Producer of **Deadliest Catch**

In 1998 I was asked by Discovery Channel to produce a TV special called *Extreme Alaska*. It would be an anthology of all things dangerous in our 49th state. I spent the next six months filming winter rescue teams, the brutal head-banging battles of mating musk ox, volcano chasers, shipwrecks and salvage companies, bush pilots, and the mystery of a body found after five years in a glacier. I filmed it all and thought I had seen it all until I went to shoot the final segment: crab fishing. I had read the great Spike Walker book, *Working on the Edge*, filled with stories of survival in the Alaskan crab fishing industry on the frigid black waters of the Bering Sea. I thought I was well prepared for my journey. Unbeknownst to my wife, who knew nothing of my plans, I doubled my life insurance policy and quietly slipped out the door for the adventure of a lifetime.

I had secured three spots on *Fierce Allegiance* from Captain Rick Mezich. Two cameramen and I jumped aboard the 183-foot vessel, a refitted Mississippi mud boat built to ferry drilling mud and pipe to the offshore oil fields south of the New Orleans Delta. It was a great choice of boat. It was big and it had a couple of extra berths and a great crew.

Heading out to sea made me think of Gilligan's expectations for his life-changing three-hour cruise. I suspected that it was going to be a hard slog for a three- or four-day adventure filled with unique visuals and great characters working in a dangerous environment. What I didn't expect was the storm that moved in quickly when we were 200 miles at sea. Within 48 hours of my departure, *Fierce Allegiance* was facing 70-knot winds and 40-foot seas. My short adventure turned into eight long, hellish days of massive weather, huge waves, and bone-chilling gusts of frigid cold. Through it all, Rick and his crew refused to stand down and worked the heavy chop. The weather doubled the days of fishing, and my crew and I continued to videotape it all. Massive waves crashing over the deck knocked the crew around like bags of potatoes in a wash cycle.

The boat went up mountainous seas and crashed down five-story slides. Full waves called "green water" rolled over the wheelhouse on several occasions, threatening to blow the windows out and send us all to the bottom. But the crew kept fishing over those long January nights, the cameras catching every move. The heavy yellow from the sodium lights bouncing off the crews' orange Grundens created a near surreal image.

The Bering Sea was relentless, pounding the boat and the crew, but the powerful deck lights couldn't cut into the water. The sea was liquid ice, 32 degrees, as cold, black, and heartless as a shark's stare. If you went overboard, your life expectancy would be only four minutes. But the brave crew ignored it all. Pot after pot, the crab kept coming. Fishing was good and the holds filled with a bounty of "bugs." There was a lot of money to be made, and I witnessed men—some barely out of high school, some seldom out of trouble, and a few mostly out of luck—earn a good chunk of cash in that week.

It wasn't all hard work. There was time for fun. I spent several days working on the deck sorting crabs between camera reloads, pushing the "keepers" into the holding tanks and the undersized to the "shit chute." I was getting pretty good at it, but the fatigue of 20-hour workdays, little appetite, and a constant dose of Asian flu slowed me down just enough for a crab to get his crusher claw around my thumb. Seventy pounds of pressure doesn't sound like much till it's clamped onto *your* appendage. It was like a 70-pound steel crowbar dropped on your thumb. It hurt like hell, and after a single yelp I spun the crab in a circle, which made his claw leg come loose from both his body and my thumb.

Weather not fit for man nor camera: Capturing the action for television involves sacrificing lots of equipment. The work is perilous, but injuries are rare.

After several days of picking crab I started to develop what crabbers call "the claw," which meant my hands wouldn't open completely. My heavy rubber gloves couldn't keep the frigid water from numbing my hands. They throbbed and wouldn't open. Captain Rick and his deck boss, Tony, had seen this many times before and offered up a rather unusual cure: Uric acid would make the pain go away. They told me to go out on deck and pee on my hands. This was the tonic. So I followed the prescription, and as I finished I looked up in the wheelhouse and caught a quick glimpse of the skipper and his deck boss having a great laugh at my expense. I was a greenhorn on their ship and I paid my dues.

There was also sadness that season. Several boats sank in the heavy seas and seven men didn't return home to their loved ones. This is the baggage carried by anyone who's worked the Bering Sea. We all know someone who hasn't returned and it lays heavy in our souls.

Something changes in a person once he's spent time at sea, and I'm no exception. When I returned to Dutch Harbor after the journey, I saw a different man in the mirror. A heavy growth of face fuzz wasn't the only thing different. I could see it in my eyes. I'd survived and even thrived on this adventure. I spent the day walking around Dutch and grunting like a feral beast. Words didn't come to me till the second day on land. I felt like I'd spit in the eye of the Devil and returned from hell to tell my story.

This spirit carries over to the 100 or so men and women that help create *Deadliest Catch*. Each October our teams of producers and cinematographers start the adventure again in the tiny town of Dutch Harbor on a small island called Unalaska, stranded in the middle of the Aleutians. Once there, our film crews will again set sight on the dented sturdy steel ships that make up the crab fishing fleet. With their hearts in their throats and their hands on their duffels, they'll bravely board and head out of port for another season. The vast Bering Sea will be waiting for them.

They'll work under brutal conditions. Freezing cold winds will whip through their constantly damp slicks, bringing chill to the bone. Black ice will creep and thicken on the deck below their nearly frostbitten feet. Giant waves will breach their workspace, threatening to sweep them into oblivion. The constant churn of the sea and the rhythm of the workers will test even the finest of our storytellers. These brave producers and cinematographers will have to keep one ear open for stories and the other for the warning buzzer. They'll keep one eye on the frame while the other eye scans the deck for danger. All of this will question their purpose and remind them how fragile their very existence is.

I am proud of all our teams who continue to go to sea, who put themselves in harm's way to follow the stories and witness the dreams fulfilled by the men and women who venture out on crab boats and together create this magically compelling, never-ending drama called *Deadliest Catch*.

It isn't easy being filmed: trying to pull pots or run a crab boat with a lens in your face and a thousand questions in your ears makes a tough job even tougher.

CHAPTER 1

THE MEN

Some were born into it *and initially hated it. Some were drawn to it from afar—and stuck with it long after the initial romance had worn off. Some are now so well-off that they could do any other job they took a fancy to—or nothing at all. But the men of* Deadliest Catch *fleet continue to return, season after season, to do the most dangerous job in the world—fishing for crab in Alaska's Bering Sea.*

So, what are they—adrenaline junkies who find the ultimate rush in fighting for their lives for high-stakes pay? Or seasoned professionals who treat their occupation as a living and take every opportunity to minimize the risk?

It seems the answer is both. These are regular working guys— consummate pros who want to "get out, get crab, and get back" as safely as possible. "We're just fishermen," they say, with great sincerity, humility—and pride. Yet they revel in risk, at sea and ashore.

On the pages that follow, they welcome you into their world, describing some of their most extreme moments—and some of their most intimate reflections—on the life-and-death business of crabbing in the Bering Sea.

The Norwegian Way
Captain Sig Hansen, F/V Northwestern

Among the most visible captains on Deadliest Catch, *Sig Hansen has one of the most complicated shoreside schedules—a steady stream of media appearances, keynote speeches, radio interviews, and public events. He speaks to packed houses at fishery expos and serves on the board of the insurance pool for the North Pacific Crab Fleet. Throughout all this he runs a complex business, fishing several seasons a year for four different types of crab.*

Sig lives with his Norwegian-born wife, June, and two daughters high on a bluff in a suburb north of Seattle, overlooking vistas of Puget Sound and the Olympic Range.

The Hansens' home is faced with limestone and set amid bronze sculptures on a tightly woven carpet of lawn. Inside, you won't find a speck of dust or smudge of dirt anywhere. The hardwood floors appear as though they were refinished yesterday. Scandinavian touches accent the decor. Highly polished contemporary paneling melds with heavily carved furniture, marble-topped coffee tables, hand-blown glass candleholders, and crystal vases filled with fresh-cut flowers.

Family photographs abound, including a large portrait of a younger Sig and June that hangs above the fireplace. Only a few small snapshots of commercial fishing subjects in glittering gilt frames provide evidence that the homeowner isn't, say, a successful medical specialist or CEO.

Sig pads about in stocking feet, dressed exactly as he appears on television, in a blue chambray shirt and jeans. His faint Norwegian accent, which is hard to notice when listening to his comments on the show, comes through more clearly in person. When asked a question, Sig stares at the veins in the marble coffee tabletop for a long moment, as though peering at a radar screen, trying to get his bearings. "Hooooo boy," he says slowly, exhaling deeply.

But once he starts talking, he is passionate and on point. He gestures extravagantly. When he describes driving Northwestern *into a heavy sea, he forms a prow with his hands, fingers coming together at the tips, and thrusts them into the air in front of him. When he explains the high- and low-water alarms on the crab holding tanks, he raises his hands way up and drops them almost to the floor.*

When the subject turns serious—injuries at sea, men lost—he appears older than he does on the show, his face slightly weathered. But as he relates a crew's prank or a joke, his boyish grin makes him look a decade or more younger than his 40-some years.

No matter the subject, Sig chooses each word carefully and delivers it forcefully. He has no trouble getting his ideas across, whether it's to a greenhorn who left his brains ashore or to a television audience.

He breaks his subject down into a string of points, then navigates from one to the next with deliberation and finesse, much like threading a crab boat down a string of pots. He clearly loves fishing, his family, his boat, his crew, and his heritage.

Sig is known for his superb safety record in this most dangerous of industries. Boat safety is at the top of his list. Dead serious about it, he speaks with the humility that comes from having survived, season after season, conditions that have sunk boats and claimed lives.

"You're a dead man."

You can have all the documents that say you are a qualified captain, and it doesn't matter. You need to be experienced on *that particular boat. [He stabs his index finger into the marble coffee tabletop with each word for emphasis.]* That's what it takes. I was 22 when I started running *Northwestern.* I was the youngest captain running a crab boat at the time. At first I mostly ran the boat in summers and got used to the vessel in calmer weather, and that helped.

Another advantage we have over most boats is that we are family members *[Sig's brother, Edgar, is his deck boss; another brother, Norman, is* Northwestern's *engineer]*, and most of the rest of the people on board have been there for many years. In fact that's the biggest advantage. Because communication is key and there is no arguing, just teamwork. And it makes it safer, period.

[Sig is particularly passionate on this point, and delivers what follows as though he is sternly lecturing a driver's-ed class on the subject of drinking and driving.]

You *cannot* take a crab boat and then go out and randomly pick five or six guys, throw them on the boat, and expect to run it safely. *It just doesn't happen.* Every boat is different. Every boat operates differently. All the decks are set up differently, so you're gonna have confusion, commotion, and something *will* happen. That's why I say the paperwork doesn't matter. I don't care if you've got papers that say you can run a giant freighter. If you're on a crab boat you've never been on before and you drive that boat into a storm, you're a *dead man.*

Sig and Edgar Hansen and *Northwestern*'s crew. A close-knit, experienced team is a crabber's best chance of survival.

[He pauses for a moment to let the point sink in. Then his voice drops back to conversational register, and he reverts to teacher mode, patiently detailing all the variables a crab boat skipper needs to be aware of to fish safely.]

You also need to know what the weather and tide is doing and then pick your gear accordingly. You need to know when to slow down and you need to know when to stop. We've been able to fish in weather in which fishing doesn't seem humanly possible. We've managed to get through it. But our game plan changes. Things slow down. We still get the job done, but we haul differently.

"It's an art."

Crab boats are all different sizes, so they all handle differently. How do you compare them? You can drive a sports car down a highway and zip through traffic. It's harder to drive a semitruck and do the same thing. My boat is 127 feet, and I have more maneuverability than a larger boat, and that can help. On the other hand the larger boats—and some of them are up to 180 feet long—have more freeboard *[they ride higher in the water, so the deck stays drier]* so they have an advantage there. Phil Harris has a larger boat than I do, but his is what we call twin-screw—it's got two engines, two propellers. You can run one engine forward and one in reverse, and it'll spin on a dime. It makes slow-speed maneuvering—the kind you need when you're picking up pots—a lot easier.

Northwestern is single-screw—one engine, one propeller—so I can't do that. I need forward momentum to turn. So I need to use lots of throttle to twist her over. The harder it blows, the more difficult it is to do that because of the pressure of the wind and waves against the hull. All I've got is the thrust of one propeller against the boat's rudder to counteract that.

No matter what size or type of boat you've got, the safety of your crew depends on your boat handling—it's an art. It's ballet. And how you do it changes constantly depending on the boat's loading, and the weather, and the sea conditions.

Say I've got all three crab tanks full of water and 59,000 gallons of fuel on board, a full load. Then I know that the boat is heavy and if I'm in the ditch—in the trough of a wave—it won't take much for water to come over the rail, for a wave to wash right over the deck. That can be deadly. It can sweep a man overboard in a heartbeat.

On the other hand if the boat is light—what we call corky, riding high in the water like a cork—then I can go in the ditch safely because the boat's going to ride high and keep the deck drier and the crew safer.

When the boat's heavy and you're in the ditch, that's when they're not safe. That's where experience comes to play— experience on that particular boat. And I know how that boat handles better than I know my car.

Every boat has its own motion, its own balance, its own way of responding to a sea. That response varies with how the boat is loaded, with its speed through the water, and with where it's riding on a particular wave. When I'm going from pot to pot I'm always adjusting the boat's speed, its direction, its angle to the waves. The waves are different sizes. They have different frequencies—different distances from crest to crest and trough to trough. Sometimes they come from slightly different directions. Sometimes waves pile on top of one another and create a superwave, a rogue wave. Sometimes they come from two directions at once. Some waves are faster and steeper than others. So you have to maneuver wave by wave. You literally take them one at a time, one hand on the jog stick *[a small lever in the pilothouse that controls the rudder angle]* and one hand on the engine throttle.

"Four-story-building-size waves . . ."

[Sig uses both controls in concert to maneuver the boat. The rudder alone doesn't steer the boat at low speed. All the rudder can do is direct the stream of water the propeller creates—a stream called

propeller wash or prop wash. So he has to artfully combine rudder angle with engine speed to give the hull just the right amount of twist for the intended turn.

Complicating his calculations are the weight of the boat; where that weight is located; how high the boat's center of gravity is; the pressure of the wind on the hull; and the size, frequency, and steepness of the seas. All these variables are constantly changing. For instance, loading varies as the boat burns fuel, fills or empties crab tanks, and takes on or off-loads gear. Windage changes even faster—in fact moment by moment—as the boat descends into the relative calm of a wave trough, then crests into what can amount to a screaming hurricane with winds of 60, 70, 80 miles per hour or more. The angle of the boat to the wind has a great effect on its responsiveness, too, as does boat speed. Like every other crab boat captain, Sig is essentially solving a complex and constantly changing physics problem every second of his watch just to keep the boat running safely.]

You're looking at a wave and you're throttling and turning, and you're doing it so that you can use the wave to your advantage. Once you know how, you can actually use a wave to help you turn the boat. When I'm on top of the wave, I know I can make a harder turn, use more rudder and throttle, and roll a little harder. That's because on top of the wave I've got more freeboard, more distance between the rail and the surface of the water. I can still keep the deck dry and the guys out of danger. I know that when I do that she'll roll harder, so I'll do that at the top of a wave.

That means she's still rolling pretty hard coming down, but that's good—because she's rolling *away* from the next wave, the big wall of water heading for the rail. When we hit that wall of water, I'm heeled over, tilting away from it, keeping the water off the deck. But I don't want to roll too much or guys will start falling off the boat. So I'll throttle back and let the boat gradually come out of the roll until I'm on the crest again. Then I'll throttle up again. As I said it's a ballet. But it's something you'll never see on TV—it's too subtle for the cameras to capture. It's me moving my hands on the controls, nudging them just a bit, watching the seas, feeling the boat.

You're looking at these three- and four-story-building-size waves and trying to feather the boat into them. You're trying to keep the boat as straight up into the wave as you can. You know you don't want to take the wave on the starboard *[right]* side of the boat because that's the working side of the boat—the rail is lower on that side, that's the side where we pull and launch the pots. Take a big wave on that side, and it'll wipe out your guys. The port *[left]* side of the boat has a higher wall around it, a higher rail. You can take a bigger wave on that side and it won't wash over the deck. But if you take the seas too much on the port side, it'll throw you off your course and it's hard to get back on your path again. So you're feathering into it—what we call jogging into it. You get to the pot and stop, let the guys do their job with the seas just a bit on the port side, then you'll maneuver after the pot is launched and the guys are done with what they need to do.

[Handling the boat is only one aspect of fishing safely. Another is communicating with the crew—often a life-or-death matter. That's because the crew is completely focused on doing specific jobs: throwing the hook around a pot buoy, running the hydraulics that haul in the pot, landing the 800-pound pot with potentially thousands of pounds of crab safely on a gyrating deck, dumping and sorting the catch, and baiting and relaunching the pot. It's up to the skipper to get the boat from pot to pot safely and to match the rhythm of the boat's movement to the rhythm of the crew's work. The crew simply can't do some tasks if the boat is pitching and rolling violently.]

You're constantly looking at the next wave coming, constantly communicating with your guys about what you're going to do, constantly assessing what they need, and trying to give it to them. If they need to do certain tasks, I may hold the boat up in the weather *[head straight into the waves to minimize the amount of side-to-side rolling the boat does]* so they can get those jobs done safely. When they're done I'll tell them, "OK, I'm heading up." That's their signal to go and hide. They'll leave the exposed part of the deck and get under shelter right behind the pilothouse and hang on.

You can do that in 20- or 30-knot winds fairly easy. If you're getting into anything above that, you've got to really watch it, depending on the size of the swells and how much the boat is weighted down.

"The boat disappears."

[Talking about heavy weather gets Sig to thinking about a situation that has sunk a lot of boats. The technical term for it is "slack tank." But his diagnosis of the problem again makes his point about how life-and-death essential it is to have an experienced hand at the helm in rough weather—and a boat that's in top shape.]

The worst time to go out is the beginning of the season. That's when the boats are weighted with fuel, weighted with pots, racing to the fishing grounds. It may be blowing 50 that day. And that's when a lot of these things happen—right when the season starts.

[Those dangerous conditions become compounded when a skipper—by definition, a boat's most experienced helmsman—takes the first, generally daylight, watch and leaves later watches or those in worse weather to rookies.]

A lot of times when a boat goes out, the captain stays awake for most of the day and then says, "I'm tired, so you guys take your watches." When the crabber *Big Valley* went down it happened at night, right after the skipper went to bed. This happens time and time again: Guys go out. The captain sits up there in the wheelhouse. The crew does their thing, getting everything ready to fish. Then the captain turns in, and you've got some guy up there that's not familiar with the boat. Pretty soon he's on the radio telling the other partner boats, "She feels kind of funny." Next thing you know the boat disappears, and everybody aboard with it.

[Sig starts to get a bit agitated again, the way he was earlier when talking about the need for experience. His normally emphatic delivery gets even more forceful until he's practically shouting.]

"She feels kind of funny." Well then *obviously* you wake up the captain immediately. *Immediately! [He jumps up from the couch and starts pacing the floor.]* If she "feels funny," you slow down and jog into it. If she "feels funny," *do* something! Don't just say she "feels funny." Don't just call your buddy up on another boat and say she "feels funny." It just *pisses me off!*

[Sig's on a real tear now, pacing rapidly, gesturing with increasing impatience and disgust. Suddenly he becomes quieter again, and his face looks older than it did just a few seconds ago.]

It just pisses me off *[he repeats quietly—sadly, even]*—because these guys probably could be here right now if the captain would take the rough watches, or if the kid at the helm would have known to throttle back, move it up *[head the boat into the waves to stabilize it]*, hit the alarm, and wake the captain.

"You get that feeling . . ."

On *Northwestern* we don't put our most experienced man up first just because he has the most seniority and wants to go to bed first. When we head out I'll say, "Well, this is what the weather's going to do, so when it's real nasty, Edgar you're up. Or Nick you're up." So that when the weather's going to be rough, we've got the most experienced person up there. Because if you've got the least experienced up there, you're in big trouble. I think that's what's happened in a lot of sinkings. The kid is at the helm, something goes wrong, he doesn't recognize it, and down they go.

[Sig elaborates. What sinks many boats, he says, is a condition called "slack tank."]

Crab boats have tanks on them to hold the crabs we catch. Most boats, including *Northwestern,* have three. They're designed to be either full of water or empty. When the tank is empty, obviously the boat is lighter. When the tanks are full—we say they're "pressed" or "down"—she's heavier. Either way the boat is stable because the distribution of weight in the boat is constant. What you don't want is a tank that has what we call free surface in it—that has some water in it but is less than full. Because then the water can slosh around in there and destabilize the boat. If you have half a tank of water, all that water sloshes from one side to another. And it can roll the boat right over.

That's especially true at the beginning of the season. The boat is heavy. You've got a full load of fuel. With all your crab pots you've got close to 200,000 pounds of steel on deck. That weight is high up, way above the waterline. It means your center of gravity is higher, so you'll roll farther and you'll roll more slowly. A fast-rolling boat is a good thing because it means she'll quickly come back to level. With a slow roll you're tipped over much longer. It's scary. You get that feeling in your gut like you're going to die.

Well, we have stability charts that tell us just how much weight we can carry where and still be seaworthy. We follow them to the letter—at least the guys who want to live do. But if you've got a slack tank, all that's out the window. You've got water that's moving inside the boat. When you roll, that water is sloshing to one side, making you roll further. When that happens, you're done. Over you go and you sink. End of story.

Slack tanks sometimes result from pump failure. We have pumps that drive seawater into the tanks to keep the crab alive when they're in there. When the pump's going it's pressing water in through pipes that run from openings under the hull into the tank. It presses the water up and out—what's called the "chute." That circulating water keeps the crab alive. You see the chute on the show when they're throwing the small crabs we can't keep overboard. That's where the stream of water that we throw them into comes from.

Anyway the pumps have circulation alarms. That's the first line of defense against a slack tank. That'll let you know if the pump's working or not. In rough weather you can actually pitch and roll so violently that you get an air bubble under the boat, and it will air-lock the pump. An air lock in the pump means it's not circulating, so now the level of the water in the tank is going down. If the circulation alarms aren't working properly, you'll never know. Until you feel it. But then most guys who haven't been in that situation don't know what it feels like. It feels like a little earthquake going through the boat. The boat actually shudders because all that water is pounding against the steel inside a tank, and that sets up a vibration in the steel hull that you don't feel until it transmits itself all the way up to the wheelhouse. If you're not familiar with it or think that it's just the waves hitting the hull, you'll never know what killed you.

That's why if the circ alarm goes off, you get up against it *[head into the waves to stop the boat from rolling]* and you get the chief *[the engineer, who maintains the boat's mechanical systems]* up immediately. But you know maybe there was no circ alarm, or maybe it got plugged with a little something. You never know And there are high- and low-level alarms in the tanks, but a lot of times they're only a foot or two from the top and bottom, and maybe that's enough slack to do it. Who knows? When you don't have pots on board you can look at the tank hatches and you'll actually see the water coming out of those hatches all the time so you know that the tank is full. But when you've got all these pots on deck, then you don't know what you're looking at.

Least Likely to Succeed

Captain Phil Harris, F/V Cornelia Marie

Every Deadliest Catch *skipper seems to have a favorite subject: Captain Sig wants to talk about boats and safety. Larry Hendricks likes to discourse on gadgets and inventions. Corky Tilley enjoys telling sea stories.*

Well, Captain Phil likes to talk about Captain Phil. That's a good thing, as his life is well worth recounting.

"Phil likes to brag a lot," warns one of his fellows with a wry smile. "So don't believe everything he says. If I say a wave is 40 feet tall, his is 90 feet. That's just the way it is."

Certainly there is nothing about Phil Harris that inclines toward understatement. Everything about him seems larger than life. He's a big man, with big tattoos, and big biceps to put them on. He drives a big pickup, one of those two-story-tall, four-wheel-drive affairs that looks like it's going to be a semi when it grows out of its rambunctious adolescence. His is a big voice, raspy from decades of heavy smoking, with a laugh that sounds like a hacksaw ripping through sheet metal. He has a reputation for talking like a sailor and for driving his boat and crew hard.

It is an image he seems eager to uphold. The man leads with his pirate tattoo and favors Harley-Davidson T-shirts with the arms ripped off (the better to display his skin art), regardless of the temperature. Even at slow speeds he guns his diesel pickup around with jabs of the throttle that make the truck buck and snort like a bull.

"One day at a time," "Easy does it," and "Don't blow a gasket" are not in Phil's vocabulary. He skippers the biggest, fastest boat in the fleet, buries the dock in his prop wash with a shove of the throttles when leaving port, and doesn't let off until the boat is full of crab. And speaking of gaskets, he blew two last year on his starboard main engine—and shattered a piston besides. Phil Harris runs hard.

Even in the relative repose of his woodsy retreat at a secluded campsite northeast of Seattle, Phil gives the impression of a restless bear, an alpha male who wants to make his status clear. Keenly aware that his fifth-wheel camping trailer—bought as a temporary residence following a divorce—may seem a bit déclassé for a high roller, he sets about correcting that misconception at once.

"Top-of-the-line everything."

I moved into here from a 5,500-square-foot house on a lake. The ceilings were 38 feet high. I got sick of it, you know? So when I got a fifth-wheel trailer I said, "Don't show me anything but the most expensive thing you've got."

You think a nice fifth-wheel is 30, 40 grand? This is $125,000. It's the top-of-the-line everything. I mean *everything*. Granite countertops. The microwave is one of those convection microwaves. The fireplace, it actually puts out heat. And the TV is big-screen HD. I've got surround sound in here—there's a stack of electronic stuff in the closet. You can put movies on. All these eyes—like that electric eye up there in the corner? I can do the remote control and turn all that stuff on and off from my leather recliner here. I've got satellite TV, satellite Internet. Everything's handmade. Built-in grandfather clock. Great stuff. I think the inside of this thing is as nice as any apartment or condo.

Could I have been OK with a 40-grand trailer? Yeah. But why spend the rest of your life driving by the dealer thinking, "I could have had the best." I've always been that way.

He pauses and reflects as he starts to make a point. And the point is not that Captain Phil Harris is the biggest, the baddest, and the best. The point is he was never supposed to be anyone at all. His bluster quickly disappears, and what's left is a candid sincerity that's downright disarming.

Phil Harris is tough enough to chew glass. But it's his big heart and keen sense of responsibility that endear him to his family and his fans.

"Raised by the police department."

I've had a lot of weird stuff happen to me. My mom died when I was 8 years old, of cancer. My dad was a fisherman. He fished up in Bristol Bay *[Alaska],* so I had to go with him. And of course I hated it because it was baseball season. I was seasick all the time. The boat was a little gillnetter—there wasn't much to it. We'd go out for a couple of months in the summertime. I hated it.

In school I was the jokester and the troublemaker. I was always in trouble with the law. In seventh or eighth grade, my dad would leave for work and I'd jump in his car and drive it to school. I'd stick all these pillows on the driver's seat, and the cops would pull me over, and they knew that my mom had died and I was kind of raising myself, and so instead of taking me down to the police station—which they did a few times—they would just take me home and call my dad and say, "Grant *[Harris, Phil's father],* you can't have your kid out driving around." I was kind of raised by the police department.

Then when I was in high school I moved out on my own when I was 15. And I would not show up for school and then I had to write my own note. And that used to piss everyone off in the school system because I'd make this big, long story about what I was doing and it drove them nuts, but there was nothing they could do because I lived on my own. That's when I was voted least likely to succeed. They didn't think I was ever going to amount to anything anyway, so just to get rid of me they fast-tracked me through high school—I did three years of high school in two years.

I graduated from high school at 16. My brother and I stayed out late one night, and suddenly I was on my way to Alaska—my brother had gotten me a job in a cannery, unloading crab boats, and I did that for about a year.

"I need to be doing something different."

I remembered that when I was in high school, one of the guys' family owned three crab boats. This kid had a brand-new Chevelle SS—a beautiful, beautiful car. I had an old '59 Volkswagen that was just barely running. I was thinking to myself: "Hell, he's driving a new car; I've got this piece of crap—I need to be doing something different."

Back then when you were a crab fisherman you could go to a bank and just walk in and say, "I want to borrow $100,000," and they'd just say, "Sign right here." They'd give you money—unsecured loans—because you were a crab fisherman. There was lots and lots of money being made.

So a boat called *American Eagle* came in to unload. They needed a kid, a greenhorn. There were probably 30 guys lined up for the job. I'm thinking to myself, "How am I going to get on this boat when all these people are trying?" So I just told the captain, "I'll work for free." And he took me.

And I thought, "Wow, I got on a crab boat!"

I called my dad and I said, "Hey, Dad"—he's been a fisherman his whole life—"I got this job." And he goes, "What?! Man, you might have bit off more than you can chew. I mean you get sick on a little boat—these guys are tough!" And I thought "What have I got to lose?"

So we're on our way to Adak—probably the roughest place in the whole world to fish, but I didn't know it. We got there and it was just flat calm and beautiful. I'm sitting on a stack of pots with the engineer, drinking beer, and I'm thinking "This is great, this crab-fishing gig."

"I didn't think you were going to make it."

Well, the next day we start setting gear, and it's blowing 120, and these pots are coming over your head, and the waves are coming over the boat. And I'm in a big pen of chopped-up herring, puking. I'm wet and cold and sick. And I thought, "Man, I just can't do this. I just can't." And I was so sick that I walked in the galley with my rain gear on and crawled up on the galley table and I'm holding on for dear life, puking my guts out. I had puke and bait and fish guts all over me, and the captain comes down and says, "Well, I didn't think you were going to make it."

And I thought, "You know what, you mother? I'm going to do this. I'm going to get up and I'm going to do this." So I went back out and I started working.

When you're new you have to work twice as hard as everybody else just to prove yourself. It took about a week and I thought I was going to die. And I'm doing this for nothing, mind you. But then the guys started feeling sorry for me 'cause they saw me trying so hard. I'm running around and I don't know what I'm doing. At first they're really cold to you 'cause you don't mean crap to them. But after a while they started making me a special meal or something because I was throwing up so bad, and they started to like me. That's what finally saved me.

I worked for 2½ months for nothing. I just kept my mouth shut and I never—*never*—brought up money. Well, one of the guys got hurt on the boat—I forget what happened to him, he broke his arm or leg or something. And so they gave me his spot, and he was a full-share guy. It was the first trip of the king crab season and in the next month I made $120,000 and I was 17 years old. And that changed everything.

"I always feel like I have something to prove."

Weird things can happen when you give a 17-year-old $100,000. The first thing I did—I found out my high school counselor, the one who led the charge on having me voted the least likely to succeed—I found out she was selling her house. She was my neighbor growing up and so she knew my situation—my not having a mom, my dad being gone a lot—and she still wanted me voted least likely to succeed.

So when I found out her house was for sale, I turned around and went down to the bank that afternoon and I told them I wanted $40,000. The asking price for her house was I think $38,000, which was big money at the time. It was a beautiful home. And I figured well, 40 grand should do it. I told them I wanted it in a paper bag. They wanted to give me a cashier's check or something but I told them no—I want it in a paper bag. In cash.

I'm 17. I've got $40,000 in stacks of bills in a paper bag and I went to the house and knocked on the door. Her husband answered, and I just walked right in and I took that bag and I dumped it out onto the kitchen table.

Well, they wouldn't sell it to me. I think they were embarrassed, you know—this smart-mouth kid with a bagful of money. And that was fine, because I didn't really want the house. But I wanted to prove the point that I *was* going to succeed.

Throughout the years—even nowadays—I always think of that. I always feel like I have something to prove. I don't think I'm a good enough fisherman, so I try harder so I can come out ahead. When you're out for three or four days and the weather is awful and most guys don't stay, I'll stay two more days to try to catch more than somebody else. Because for some reason I feel like I'm not as good as they are. So that "unsuccessful" label was the motivator that I've never forgotten. They labeled me least likely to succeed. And look at me now.

Phil has a different message for the cops who were always picking him up for some infraction or other when he was in high school.

A few years ago I had a big party at my house, and I invited these cops that saved me when I was younger, and they showed up. One of them is now the chief detective for the police department. He sat down, and we talked, and he looked around at my big lake house and everything I had and he started crying. He couldn't believe that I had made it and that he'd had a hand in it. It was a neat moment.

I would do just the stupidest stuff when I was a kid, but when I was in trouble with the law I always was respectful. He got teary-eyed because he helped me get to where I am today. A lot of those guys were like family in the end. They all had a little part in getting me where I'm at.

"I don't want to be down here. I want to be up there."
On the crab boats though, Phil made his own opportunities.

When I was working on deck, I always paid attention to what we were doing. I used to ask questions—how does this work and how does that work. And during the long runs I'd be the only one who'd go upstairs and volunteer to take wheel watches while the rest of the guys were sleeping. I thought, "Well, I'm down here freezing my ass off. I've been up for three days. I'm tired. I'm cold. I'm hungry."

Then I go up there in the wheelhouse. It's warm. The skipper's listening to music, he's got life by the tail and he's making three times as much as I am. What is wrong with this picture? I don't want to be down here. I want to be up there. So I would go up and take watches when nobody else would.

So finally on my 21st birthday they let me run that boat. All the crew is a lot older than me, and they didn't think this was cool at all. Well, I worked my tail off to get there and I was really good on deck, but in the grand scheme of things, I didn't know what I was doing, and the crew knew it. A couple of them wanted to quit. But the boat owners said, "Look, we're giving this kid a boat because we think he can do it and you guys have been with us a lot of years—you guys help him in any way you can."

And it turned out they were pretty cool. I went out and I was lucky enough to catch a few crab and it worked out OK. But I had my times. There is a learning curve to running a boat, and my very first trip I almost rolled the damn boat over. I came into Dutch Harbor, and when you come into Dutch Harbor you come right in front of the Elbow Room and you have to make a hard right turn to go into the cannery.

The cannery radioed me and said, "Let your tanks down, the ground crew is waiting for you," and blah, blah, blah. So I make that corner with half a tank of water and the boat rolled right over and laid on its side. I had to do a lap to get it back upright. I made a big boo-boo. I'm right in front of town and I felt about this big.

One season right at the beginning, the average catch was 80,000 pounds and I had 15,000. That's the only time that I've ever really bombed. That feeling, I'll never forget it. That was my second motivator. I never, *ever* want to wind up like that again. You're pulling into the dock and all the other boats made X dollars and your crew didn't even make enough to fly in and out. That's only happened one time in my career, and that was enough.

I'm responsible for everyone on the boat and their families. I have guys working for me that have been with me on and off for 25 years. We don't change crews a lot. I try to be a fair guy to work for. The guys who leave I train and they go on to run other boats—I've done that with three guys now. And they're all highly successful in the way they handle their crews too.

God, that was a long time ago. I feel like an old man.

He pauses for a moment.

Here's something that scared me when I watched it.

He reaches for the remote and aims it at the all-controlling electric eye.

Now I don't watch a lot of television, but I happened to watch this one show and I'll probably watch it a lot just to remind me what the guys on deck actually go through. Because I usually leave it up to them to call it if it's too tough to fish. I'll call it if the boat isn't handling right. But if the boat's fine and the pots are lined up, then it's a matter of just how tough it is for them. Most of the time they like to fish when it's really bad out. They think it's fun. But when you're looking at it from the wheelhouse, you're looking down. I didn't see it from their angle, and it was amazing to me. Look at this . . .

He hits a button and the big high-definition screen comes to life with the voice of Mike Rowe, the Deadliest Catch *narrator:*

"Sixty-six miles to the south of the *Northwestern,* Captain Phil on the *Cornelia Marie* is halfway into setting a 20-pot string when he runs smack into a set of heavy rollers on the leading edge of a storm."

Captain Phil leans forward, interrupting the show's audio, his gaze locked to the screen.

"That is a lot of water, man," *Phil says quietly, watching a wave slam into the port side of the boat. Spray flies back and momentarily obliterates the view of the crew,* "and you've got guys working out there."

He's suddenly tense as a cat and is clearly reliving the moment. He's almost bracing himself in his recliner for the impact of the next crushing wave.

"*Focus is key, and Phil is in no mood for company," continues the narration, which booms through concealed speakers in every corner of the trailer's living room.*

The camera focuses on a considerably more haggard Captain Phil than the one watching the show. "Absolutely," *he's saying to the* Deadliest Catch *film crew in a dead-serious voice that's a cross between an order and a plea.* "I don't want anything going on, not even chitchat when we set this stuff. I don't want any interruptions. No chitchat. The waves come up, have a tendency to go to the back of the boat, and wipe out whoever's standing there."

The narrator: "These are the worst possible conditions for an exhausted deckhand to be working in."

"Well, it's a scary business right now, I can tell you that," *says Phil soberly. Mentally and emotionally he's back in the pilothouse. He rapidly, almost unconsciously, lights a cigarette without taking his eyes off the screen. As another wave hits, he winces and seems to be reaching for the throttles to control the boat.*

"Tens of thousands of gallons of water crash over the rail, moving the 800-pound pots like Tinkertoys," says narrator Mike Rowe.

"You see," *says Phil,* "you got guys going in the pot—"

"But with just a handful of pots left, the deckhands will tough it out," interrupts Rowe.

Everybody's life is at stake. Phil points at a dot on the screen—one of his sons has crawled into a pot on the launcher to bait it. "Josh is in there. A wave could take out anybody. You're going to see a big one coming."

"Challenging the Bering Sea is never a wise move," intones Rowe.

Suddenly a huge lump of water the size of a low-rise apartment complex appears on the edge of the screen, heading for the boat.

"That is one big-ass wave," *says Phil, his gaze still riveted to the images on the screen.*

"A 20-foot monster roars toward the men," resumes the narrator. "Phil counts the deckhands. By the grace of God no one's been sucked back into the sea. There are just two more pots, one on deck and one in their launcher."

That last wave destroyed a $30,000 camera downstairs. See those waves hit the house? They make such a noise. It's as loud as a jet airplane taking off when those waves hit the ceiling. And that's three stories up. The house is 35 feet tall. Listen to it! It's deafening.

He flicks off the TV and leans back, reorienting himself. He stubs out the cigarette and exhales deeply.

You know what that's like? That's like—oh, maybe taking your kids down at 11 at night, giving them a couple of flashlights, and telling them to go play in the middle of the freeway. I mean that's just what it's like for us. This is big-time weather, man. This is big-time weather and anything can happen. I look at that clip sometimes just to get the guys' perspective on deck of what they are going through. I learn from it. I'm always learning. Always paying attention and learning.

But that one there was a little much.

Johnathan Hillstrand

Andy Hillstrand

The Wild Man and the Cowboy
Captains Johnathan and Andy Hillstrand

The Hillstrand brothers are the definition of colorful.

Johnathan, with his five days growth of beard and wind-blown, biker hair looks as if he's just climbed off his nitrous-fueled Harley Fat Boy and into the wheelhouse of Time Bandit.

His brother, Andy, wears a cowboy hat. On deck.

The two of them split the duties of captain on Time Bandit. *Johnathan fishes king crab; Andy, opilio.*

Johnathan is the self-described bad boy. "I spend all my money," he says, "on whiskey and women."

Andy is the clean, quiet one. "I shave," he confesses. "I do the paperwork."

The TV cameras love Johnathan for his tendency to play tricks on his fellow captains, such as the time he tied bags of flour to another boat's pot lines, then stood by to film the result: One "flour bomb" after another exploded as the pot was hauled.

"It turned all the guys on deck into Pillsbury dough boys," recalls John with his trademark raspy cackle. "The boat looked like it was made out of plaster when we were done. It turned everything white. We were laughing so hard, we cried."

Cameras are also fond of what Andy calls John's "Snidely Whiplash laugh"—usually accompanied by an impishly evil grin that betrays his intention to play yet another prank on a fellow boat.

"I'm gonna get Phil next season!" John says. More raspy cackling. "He thinks he's got better tricks than me. But I've got the old tricks and the new ones. I'm going to do 10 tricks on one pot of his. I can't tell you what they are yet. Just watch."

The media, on the other hand, often find Johnathan to be a difficult interview. Not because he's shy but because he has, as he describes it, "straight pipes from brain to mouth." He'll say anything about anyone. "Don't print that!" is perhaps his most frequently uttered line—always g something spectacularly profane or slanderous.

season you can typically find Johnathan, as another skipper

ed, "anywhere there are motorcycles and women."

"For John," the skipper added, "women are always in season."

Andy has the air of a college professor by comparison—cowboy hat notwithstanding. He's been married to the same woman for 22 years—something of a record among crab fishermen, whose constant absence, high stress, and reputation for partying make them prime candidates for divorce. Andy can talk at length without uttering a single four-letter word and has nothing but good to say about everybody.

Off the boat Andy gravitates to his 17-acre horse ranch in southern Indiana—about as far from the ocean as you can get. He's a practitioner of what he calls "natural horsemanship."

"It's using the way the horse communicates to have them do what you want," Andy explains. "I act like another horse would act. With horses there's a pecking order. What the horse is looking for is a leader, so you act like a leader. You're a leader, but you're fair. Once you learn how horses communicate, you can train a horse to do anything you want to do. Humanely—no whips, no spurs."

Yep: Andy the crab-boat skipper is a horse whisperer.

But beneath these stylistic differences, the brothers Hillstrand are remarkably in sync. There's no role-confusion, no arguing: When they're fishing king crab, John's word is law. For opilio season Andy sits in the skipper's chair and John becomes one of the crew— although a privileged member, who pretty much gets to pick and choose his duties.

They're also unified in their highly professional approach to running a crab boat. They skipper a very tight, well-organized, highly trained, safe, productive vessel, and they intend to keep it that way. In spite of their flamboyance, "There's not a lot of drama on our boat," John says.

"We don't yell," Andy adds, "unless it's serious."

Captain John checks the state of the seas during a haul.

Andy: We grew up in Homer, Alaska, fishing summers with our dad in a little gillnetter. He designed *Time Bandit*—sketched the whole thing out on boat napkins. We all went to the yard and helped build it, and he sold it to us. We've been crab fishing now for 27 years. I've only missed two seasons; John's just missed one. John and I are really good friends. Our younger brother, Neal, is the cook and engineer who keeps us fed and keeps everything running.

John: It's a beautiful boat. It's the number-one stability-tested boat. It's like a flat-bottom skiff. The only thing you could have more stable out there would be a barge. We're like Noah's ark: not real fast, but we can go through anything God can throw at us.

It's not always pleasant. On the show we're rolling 30, 40 degrees sometimes, but the camera's bolted to the boat, so it's rolling with us. It looks like we're just sitting there talking, but it can be a miserable mother out there. You can't put anything down. Eggs fly out of the pan—they pretty much scramble themselves. Bacon grease flies out and catches on fire. When it's minus-40 degrees, you have to eat four or five meals a day just to keep warm.

I once said, "If I get hit by another plate of food, I'm going to quit." Right then—I'm wearing a clean, white T-shirt—three plates of spaghetti and everyone's juice and salad hit me right in the chest. I quit for about 10 minutes before I rehired myself.

Andy: But compared with other boats, living conditions on our boat are like a five-star hotel. We have queen-size Sealy Posturepedic mattresses in the bunks. Most of 'em just have foam. My dad said, "Why build yourself a $3 million boat and then lie down on a piece of foam?" We can sleep and wake up again and not feel like someone bent us in half. We've got a sauna on the boat, dishwasher, washer-dryer, nice stoves. We live good.

But it doesn't make the work any easier. We never used to talk about how bad we hurt. That was showing weakness. My dad always said, "Never say die. Never say quit." Now with the show we're having to describe to people how it is. You can't feel your hands, you work for so long. Your arms go numb—they feel like lead weights. It's the same when you're in the wheelhouse. The hardest time to stay awake is right before dawn. When the sun comes up, it feels like sandpaper in your eyes, but then you're good for the rest of the day. Slap some water on your face, drink a potload of coffee . . .

John: We fished when we were kids. It's in your blood. I see these guys say, "I'm ready; I can do this." They can't. They're used to eight hours of sleep. He'll be crying like a baby in three days and sucking his thumb and whining for his mama. On the other hand, you can have a little tiny guy like Jake Harris, who grew up in the fishery; he knows what he's doing.

Andy: The biggest guy in the world doesn't necessarily do best. Little

Fishing involves hard physical work in a harsh environment, but it's the mental aspect that presents the greatest challenge to the crew, says John Hillstrand.

guys can do the job. Mentally you just have to want it real bad.

John: It's *all* mental out there. It's a lot of heart and soul. Sometimes you're staying up for three or four days. We're not on drugs out there. I get that all the time—people asking me, "How do you *really* stay up that long?" We've been conditioned into this kind of life. We can sit for two hours and work for 12. You'd be surprised at what the human body can do.

Andy: That's where the pranks come in. You work so hard, you want to have a good time. Being the captain you've got to be a psychologist too. If the crew's down, you've got to think of a pep-me-up. Up there you've got nothing to do but think. John likes to throw seal-bombs *[firecrackers]* at us. He put one on a frying pan once and blew the thing up. It scared the crap out of me. Then he laughs like Snidely Whiplash!

John: Heh, heh, heh!

Andy: He's a good brother. I've got some of the best brothers in the world. We're older now, everything gets in the groove, we don't fight about it. We're all real happy doing what we do. I'm the paperwork guy, John's our resident hell-raiser.

John: It gets you through the bad times. You think about little stuff like what you've done to the guys. I like to tape up the sink faucet in the galley. That way when you turn the water on, the pot-sprayer sprays you right in the chest. Half the time I'll forget I've done it. I'll run downstairs to wash up and I'll get myself! We shut off the hot water sometimes when guys go to take a shower. On deck when a guy's busy, we'll tie his leg to the sorting table. Then he goes to run off to do something else, he hits the end of the line and falls on his face. Anything we can think of for a laugh.

'Cause there's plenty of bad times. Crab fishing's either heaven or hell. You're either pulling full pots or pulling blanks, and it can go from one to the other really fast out there. You only think about the heaven if you're going to come back for the next trip.

I've had a lot of friends die. Everywhere I go I'm thinking, "That guy died there, this guy died here." It gets to you a little bit.

Andy: I have four friends who have died on other boats. We've had guys cut the tips of their fingers off, stuff like that. My chiropractor says I have the back of a 70-year-old man. But we're all alive.

John: You're only as good as the guys on deck. We bring out guys that ain't going to get seasick. Misfits make good TV, but they don't make good fishermen. Maybe I ought to hire six of'em and I'd be the only boat they'd show! It'd be *my* show!

Andy: We've got to really watch the Discovery guys though. They got their eyes shoved in a viewfinder. You got to watch those guys' backs, show 'em all the spots where they could get hurt: "Don't stand over here because if the pot falls out of the launcher, you're dead."

John: We did save a guy that one time. Pulled a crewman from another boat out of the water. That was a once-in-a-lifetime triumph, a pretty personal moment for me. I can't watch that episode without tearing up. Another minute in the water and he'd have been dead.

I've pulled dead guys out of the water before. I had a guy take his last breath right in front of me, but when we got him onboard, he was dead. Phil's done the same thing. It's pretty cool when you can redeem yourself and save a guy.

Because if you're in the water without a survival suit, you won't make it five or 10 minutes. In a survival suit you're good for five or six hours. In a raft you can survive overnight. It's not long. That's why we do so many drills. We train, train, train for those kinds of situations. You can't do the drills enough. We train to get the crane, get a life sling, get a survival suit on and pull the guy in. Even if he doesn't make it, the body is important. It's closure. If you don't have a body, the family's thinking, "Maybe he made it, maybe he swam to shore somewhere."

Andy: That guy who didn't make it had seven kids. He'd been fishing his whole life. And they thanked us for bringing the body back.

John: A lot of people die out there from greed or desperation. You do stupid stuff, carry too much ice and you get top-heavy and roll over, whatever. Then you're maydaying, and if you're screwed on a hundred-foot boat, you sure don't want to get into a little life raft.

Andy: What kills people is complacency. You think, "I've been doing this for 20-some years," and you don't check the engine room. There's a leak you don't know about and you go down. We've pretty much weeded that out now. All the boats in the fleet now are top-notch boats. But even so we've come close.

John: We took a wave in Unimak Pass *[in the Aleutian Islands, connecting the Bering Sea with the Pacific Ocean]*. It was 130 feet tall with a 30-foot white-water breaker on top.

Andy: White water is like skiing in powder. There's so much air in the water, you sink. You're actually underwater, the whole boat. When that wave wrapped around the pilothouse windows, I thought, "This is what it's like to die."

John: We went so deep, you couldn't see daylight. It was really, really dark. I don't know how deep we were. We were going full-bore forward, and I'm not sure whether that pushed us deeper or helped us climb out—you couldn't even tell which way was up. The hit was so violent that everything in the galley went flying— the refrigerator, everything. The microwave put a square hole in a door that was 28 feet across the boat!

Andy: Guys were standing on the side of walls, alarms were going off…

John: Water was pouring into the engine room through the fresh-air vents, and the bilges were pumping full bore. Even so the engine room was filling up. The auxiliary *[generator]* didn't go out, thank God, or we would have lost steering. If the mains suck water down the intake, the motors would have died, and then we'd have been screwed. It was a half hour before my legs stopped shaking enough that I could stand.It was that close.

Why do I keep doing it? I don't *have* to do it. I have investments and properties. I'm pretty well set up. But it's in your blood. You gotta go. Not to go out one season—it's like missing a hunt or something. I'll never retire. When I get old I'll at least fish salmon in the summer. I'll probably die out there in my little salmon boat—not because I sank, just because of old age!

The Seasoned Pro

Captain Jerry "Corky" Tilley, F/V **Aleutian Ballad**

Corky ("The only people who call me Jerry are lawyers and doctors," he says.) Tilley is a fisherman's fisherman. Even ashore he is never far from a boat. He lives in a small apartment on top of his fishing shed in the Washington seaside village that has been his lifelong home. The steel shed towers over the modest ranch house Corky bought with Alaskan crab money in 1976 and which he now rents out. Orderly stacks of crab pots, fish totes, nets, and buoys surround the shed.

The shed's cavernous interior contains Corky's 30-foot gillnetter, a sleek-looking fiberglass fishing machine he bought with the proceeds of another Alaska season back in 1979. A huge aluminum spool of fine, almost invisible gillnet dominates the boat's deck. More nets pile in corners like snowdrifts. Big chunks of machinery—pot haulers, hydraulic pumps, and other deck hardware—await repair or refitting. The place is redolent with the faint but pleasant smell of barnacles and drying twine.

A two-story stairway leads to Corky's living quarters. Anyone expecting crab-boat-cabin slovenliness is in for a surprise: The apartment, which Corky designed after he divorced and his children grew up and left home, is tidy and efficient. Photographs and paintings of nautical scenes hang on the walls.

The focal point of the living room is a large binnacle—a classic, varnished wood cabinet that houses a ship's compass—centered beneath a broad window overlooking the ocean. A settee is placed against the wall behind the binnacle almost exactly where you would find the pilothouse bench aboard a crabber. Corky likes to stretch out on the settee, a cup of coffee in hand, and tell sea stories.

Ashore he often wears the same gear he does at sea: a well-broken-in "Big Mac" insulated flannel shirt and a pair of jeans—the uniform of the working fisherman. His frank, open face and relaxed, unguarded manner make him instantly likable.

"Didn't have a choice."

I'm a third-generation fisherman. My stepdad was a deckhand when I was little. When I got to be 10 or 11, he bought an old halibut boat, the *Orbit*. I went up to Seattle with him to bring it home. I got so sick that trip, I thought I'd never get on a boat again in my life.

But I did of course. I'd go out trolling on *Orbit* with my stepdad. I'd be sick for three days, then I'd start coming out of it. That happened every trip. I got sick for 10 years. I still get a bit nauseous if it's rough and I haven't been out in a while.

When I was 15 or 16 I got home half an hour late one night. My mom said if I couldn't live by her rules, then I'd have to move out, so I did. I had to support myself, so my uncle let me use a 17-foot cedar skiff to gillnet with. I had a 50-fathom *[300-foot]* chunk of net that I'd pull by hand.

The boat leaked so bad that every morning it'd be sunk at the dock. Only the net would be floating, and the gunwales *[the top edges of the hull]* would be just barely above water. I'd get the first few buckets out by sitting on the dock. I could see the bay right through the sides of that boat.

When I was out fishing I'd pull some net, pick some fish, bail the boat, pull some more net. The water was usually halfway to my knees. I'd gillnet before school—go out, catch the tide, make a drift, and then head in to school. I didn't have time to change or shower so I'd go directly from the boat to school in hip boots and a Big Mac, smelling like fish and soaking wet.

When gillnetting season was over, I'd fill in crab fishing on local boats. I'd be so sick, I'd be puking in the bait jar. But my apartment cost me 50 bucks a month. I had to do it to make a living. I really didn't have a choice.

I first got the Bering Sea bug in 1973. I was coming in from fishing and saw this huge, brand-new steel boat off-loading Dungeness crab at the cannery. It was *Ocean Leader*, one of the first ultramodern crab boats. The crew invited me into the galley for dinner. It was the biggest, fanciest thing I'd ever seen. The insides were plush, the wheelhouse stairs went on forever. I was amazed. I'd been living in squalor compared to these guys. They started telling me stories of the Bering Sea, fishing king crab. I was hooked.

My real dad, Jerry Tilley Sr., lived in Dutch Harbor and ran Vita Seafoods. I told him I wanted to go fishing on the Bering Sea. A couple years later he got me a job on *Intrepid,* a brand-new crab boat. I packed a sea bag, got on an airplane, and landed in Dutch.

There were no balloons and confetti when I got there, that's for sure. I had to crawl onto the boat while it was off-loading crab via a little narrow catwalk with crab gurry raining down on me. I was soaking wet and covered in stinking crab guts, and so was all my gear. I was miserable before I even hit the boat. The crew wasn't happy to see me either. The captain had fired one of their buddies, and I was his replacement. I'm thinking, "What am I doing here?"

Corky Tilley still has an affection for the leaky 17-foot skiff that started his fishing career more than three decades ago.

Corky in his native habitat: the wheelhouse of a fishing boat.

"I am so out of here!"

After we unloaded we ran 12 hours. It was storming, and I'm on deck chopping bait just sicker than a *dog*. I'm totally green for king crab, I have no idea what I'm doing. They start yelling and screaming at me. I thought I had died and gone to hell. It was the most miserable I had ever been in my whole life. I'm thinkin', "I am so out of here. I hate everybody, they hate me…"

But I get in from my first trip, I find out I've made a couple grand. I can't believe it. I think, "Well, I can handle this for a couple grand." After that, I was so tired of being yelled at that I really concentrated, tried my hardest to be one step ahead of 'em. So I fell into the groove.

After I was worth my salt, they started to be a little nicer to me. I ended up being great friends with all those guys and am to this day. By the end of the season I was a high roller. When I got home I bought a new pickup, and a three-wheeler, and this house out here.

"Neanderthal half-wits."

[Next season Corky landed a spot as a full-share deckhand on a new crab boat, Westward Wind. *The boat grossed more than $1 million*

in its first season. Corky's take was $50,000 or about what a senior business manager earned at the time. Corky was still in his early 20s. But unlike some of his peers, Corky didn't blow his check on partying and fast cars. Perhaps the memory of fishing by hand in a half-sunk skiff tempered his spending, or perhaps it was that he was soon married with two kids. Instead of a Corvette, he bought his gillnetter.]

Every time I made money I invested some of it in something with lasting value: a house, a boat I could go out and make more money with. Some of the guys I went to high school and fished with in the early days, they're riding a bicycle through town now. They got nothin'. Drank it all. I don't partake in that kind of action. Early on I partied with the best of them, but if I've got some free time in Dutch Harbor now, I get a good night's rest. A lot of guys get smash-faced drunk and it's part of the program. It costs you a lot of money, and you feel like dirt the next day. It's fun to hang out and hear the bull, but we're not a bunch of drunk Neanderthal half-wits. A lot of us treat fishing as a business and a way to make a living.

"Nothing comes close."

[For the next 15 years, Corky worked eight months of the year on Bering Sea crab boats, working his way up to mate and then captain, coming home summers to gillnet right out of his hometown port so he could spend time with his family. Eventually he bought his 50-foot fishing boat, which he fished for Dungeness, blue crab, and black cod, sometimes making up to $100,000 in an eight-day season. But the allure of the Bering Sea keeps him coming back to Alaska.]

Down here fishing it was a cakewalk, I could do anything they could dish out—it was a walk in the park. You actually come home every few days. Hell, a lot of these guys out here were day boats. And the weather—nothing comes close to the Bering Sea.

The Crab Wizard
Captain Keith Colburn, F/V **Wizard**

Unlike most of the Deadliest Catch *captains, Keith Colburn did not grow up fishing—or even anywhere near the water. A self-described ski bum from the resort town of Lake Tahoe he ended up in Kodiak, Alaska, after an adventuresome friend suggested they give fishing a try. Drawn by the lure of adventure, the ocean, and the physical challenge, he's been fishing for more than two decades. He worked his way up from greenhorn deckhand to captain and boat owner, earning the respect of fishermen whose families have been salty for generations.*

Captain Keith is a bear of a fellow, stocky and muscular, with an energy level that has only one setting: full throttle. Like the auxiliary power generators aboard his boat, Wizard, *you get the impression that he's someone who needs to run with a load on or he'll burn up his own wiring with too much untapped power.*

When Keith meets someone, he starts talking immediately, words and phrases tumbling out like water over a fall. He interrupts himself constantly, as though there were three or four Keiths in there, each trying to make sure the others don't leave out some crucial detail.

He approaches fishing with an entrepreneurial zeal for taking big risks in an industry that's already risky and is undergoing constant regulatory change. Through a combination of extraordinary luck, skill, and financial nerve, Keith leveraged his way into the ownership of two crab boats at a time when the fleet was shrinking rapidly and has made the investment pay off handsomely—only to pour the profits into yet more investments in gear and crab quotas.

Keith lives like an entrepreneur too—in a big, contemporary home high above a secluded lake near Seattle. There's a new S-class Mercedes in the garage sporting a vanity plate that reads PECHEUR— "fisherman" in French. Keith's wife, Florence, who was born in France, gets to drive that; Keith commutes to the boat in a more pedestrian SUV. He and Florence run the business together; he skippers and manages the boats, she keeps tabs on regulatory matters and helps with business strategy while Keith's on the water. Off-hours they're just as active: Keith arrived on deck for the start of one season fresh from a bicycle tour of eastern Europe.

Up in Wizard's *wheelhouse, his chart plotter—a computerized navigation device that can plot a boat's position on an electronic chart—is a dense web of past seasons' fishing courses, pot locations, and typed-in commentary. Keith logs each pot's catch. Inconceivable as it may seem, Keith can tell when and where* Wizard *caught every single crab it brought to the dock. He knows within a few feet where he's run his pot strings—not only last season, but the season before and the season before that. And he's logged the catches of all the research vessels that drop their pots on a widespread grid throughout the Bering Sea—the data used to calculate the size of the crab population every year and to determine crab quotas. Unlike many captains, who edit their information to prevent overload, Keith mops it all up and stores it in his multiplex memory.*

Ironically, whim, gut feel, and a growing web of superstitions regularly trump all this scientifically gathered, technologically plotted data. If anything, Keith pays more attention to them than his bearings and numbers.

In addition to the bank of radar and computer monitors that surround Wizard's *helm station, you notice little pieces of evidence that science and technology aren't the only forces guiding this multimillion-dollar fishing vessel and its hyperintelligent, highly driven, extremely successful skipper.*

Here's Keith in the wheelhouse explaining the boat to an increasingly mystified visitor from shore:

Yeah, when you get all this stuff fired up and running, it's a pretty major electronic command center. We've got a radar, a black-box sounder, a back-up radar, a plotter, a back-up plotter—everything's redundant. We've got two GPSs, two side-bands, two VHFs, two depth sounders, pretty much two of everything. Plus a gyrocompass and a

Ski-bum turned crab-fishing powerhouse Keith Colburn fuels his enterprise with an off-the-charts level of energy and intensity.

magnetic compass. We don't use those much anymore, but we keep 'em around in case the GPS satellites get shut off for some reason. That gyro's about a $40,000 compass.

So what's that battered, stained Styrofoam cup, cradled in a handmade wooden holder next to the captain's chair?

That's, uh, my lucky Cup-o-Noodles spittoon.

*"Your **what**?!"*

My lucky spittoon. I chew incessantly when I'm fishing. I try not to but I do. It's just a bad habit. When I'm driving the boat, I'm doing it all the time. And I've had some good seasons using that particular type of Styrofoam cup for a spittoon, so that's all I use now.

You're kidding, right? All these computers...

Nope. Dead serious. I was out of Cup o' Noodles one year fishing red crab. Didn't have one, just had a regular coffee cup or something for a spittoon, and I'm sitting here driving and I'm on nothing. I'm just stinking it up. But I've still got a bunch of gear out there that I haven't checked yet. My brother Monte was on the *Sea Fisher*, and I'm on the radio to him, going, "You got to get over here, this is an emergency. You've got to get me a Cup o' Noodles."

He's going, "Whaaat? No way, I'm not going out of my way to give you a Cup o' Noodles."

I go, "I *need* a Cup o' Noodles!"

No sooner did that Cup o' Noodles hit that spot right there, than we went from zeroes to thirties and forties. From nothing to great fishing like that!

So you say is it all just fun and games, stuff like that? I mean, can I survive fishing without that Cup o' Noodles sitting there? Yes! Am I going to? No way! Would you? Why? If it's worked, don't change it, right?

So any other lucky... amulets aboard?

Oh, yeah! I have my lucky pencil that I write my bearings down with. I use only a certain kind of pencil for writing down all my stuff—a 9-millimeter mechanical pencil that clicks. *Have* to use that. I got my little box my daughter made me to hold stuff. It's right here. I got my lucky rock with a smiley face on it. I hold it and rub it for luck, and now the smiley face is all worn off. Most things though, they have to do with what *not* to do, with stuff that brings bad luck.

Such as?

In the galley all the coffee cups are on hooks, right? You gotta have 'em all hanging the same way. If they're going every which way, that's bad luck.

So you'll actually rearrange…?

Oh yeah. Bad news. And split pea soup—don't make split pea soup when you're out at sea. That's a big no-no. And honeys. Do you know honeys, these little plastic bears they sell honey in? Don't bring them on board. And suitcases! Absolute, big-time no-no. Don't even *think* about bringing a suitcase on my boat.

The *Deadliest Catch* camera crew came on board, and they had some suitcases. I got on the loud hailer and said "Hey! *OFF* with the suitcases."

And they're like, "It's my gear. I need this stuff."

I said, "Unload it then and bring the stuff with you. But don't bring that suitcase on my boat."

And they ask one of the guys on deck: "Is he serious? He can't be serious!"

And they go, "Yeah, he's serious! Get it off!"

Horses. You can't bring a horse on a boat. Bad luck. We don't even say the "H" word on a boat. In fact I can't believe I just said it. It's like whistling in the wheelhouse.

You can't do that either?

Oh no. You'll whistle up a storm. My first season on a boat, I walked into the wheelhouse and the music was on and I started whistling along and the captain looked at me and went, "Don't do it!"

I go, "What's that all about?"

He goes, "You're going to whistle up a storm."

Sure as hell, eight hours later we got into a major blow. We were towing three smaller boats, and all of them broke loose. We had to retrieve the boats, anchor up for the evening—it was nasty out. Because I was whistling in the wheelhouse, it was my fault. So obviously from that day, you don't hear *me* whistling in the wheelhouse. And I don't particularly care to have anybody else do it either."

Superstitions have served *Wizard* well, according to Captain Keith Colburn, who stays unwaveringly mindful of seafaring traditions.

So this is serious stuff. This isn't just for fun?

No, I take it very seriously. I pretty much take on every superstition there is. The thing is I disregard the females-on-board thing, because you have to, right? I mean if I got freaked out every time a girl walked on this boat, I would be doomed. Because 10 percent of the time or 20 percent of the time you're going to have an official observer on board taking crab weights and sizes. You don't have a choice as to whether it's a male or female. It's whoever the department decides to put on you. So if you're stuck with a woman on board, you're stuck with a woman on board.

And they don't respect the tradition. You can't say, "No, I'm sorry, I can't have a woman because . . ."

Ha! Nah! They'd just laugh you right out of the office."

So you do the left-handed Swedish circle thing like John Hillstrand if you have to leave on a Friday then, right?

No, that's bogus. He just made that up. But you know what?
I guarantee you long after the cameras are gone, he'll still be doing that turn…."

…and believing it?

Oh yeah!

So he made it up and then he believes it?

Absolutely!

The birth of a new superstition.

Right! There are new ones all the time. One of the scientists in fish and game had some dice on her desk. You'd roll them and they'd make up a phrase. She had them there just for fun. Well I rolled them, and they said "Become one in a faraway place." So that year I fished waaaay up north, farther than anyone else. And I had a great season. Now I roll those dice every year.

What do you attribute this to? Who is speaking through the dice or through these various superstitions?

I have no idea. But you know what? I've had a good run of luck and I'm not changing it. Bottom line.

The Idea Man
Captain Larry Hendricks, F/V Sea Star

Larry Hendricks lives in a modest-size contemporary home with big glass windows that look out on the sparkling blue water of a small lake in a Seattle suburb.

Larry loves water. He swims every day in season. He's built a waterfall, a rock-lined stream, and a pond on his property. He stocks the pond with fish from the lake. An elaborate series of decks, stairways, and ramps leads from his house to the water. His crew built them. Larry just kept the men on the payroll and put them to work in his yard.

The deck has more grades, slopes, angles, and turns than one might think a deck could possibly have. "It got kind of boring, really, building this compared to working on a boat," says Larry. "We tried to make it interesting."

The closer you get to the house, the more obscure and complex the design becomes until it devolves into a composition of half-removed siding and half-constructed porch. Larry was in the middle of installing a new second-floor deck when life got complicated— Deadliest Catch *appearances, interviews, lots of traveling.*

Larry himself is often similarly disheveled: He has a penchant for wearing unbuttoned Hawaiian-print shirts, shorts, and going barefoot. He shaves infrequently, and his hair tends to stick out at Einsteinian angles. The low-maintenance look lets him concentrate on other things. "I don't own a jacket," he volunteers. "I'd only lose it anyway. I'd leave it somewhere. I've got too much going on in my mind."

There's ample evidence of that. Larry is well-known to Deadliest Catch *fans as the captain who turned his boat,* Sea Star, *into a robotic wonder, heavily modifying the crab-catching equipment for what he affectionately calls his "geriatric crew."*

"He's got it set up so you don't so much as have to bend over on that boat," says another crab skipper admiringly. "A crane lifts the pot

right over to the sorting table. Larry designed it all."

What viewers may not know is that Larry is a technical consultant to the Deadliest Catch *production team and acts as a liaison between the production crew and the fishing fleet. He even designs special gear and equipment to help the show get shots that otherwise would be impossible to record.*

His inventiveness is seemingly limitless. As he talks he spews ideas, stories, recollections, and information with almost volcanic force. It's as though there's a 16-track tape playing in his mind, and he's trying to get it all out through a single mouth.

Larry doesn't stand on ceremony. He likes to be comfortable. When talking he's inclined to flop down on a couch, filling it end to end. He's a human mountain range, one with a very large technical vocabulary and a tendency to stream-of-consciousness monologues. If you can follow what he's saying, he's an oracle. If not, he's still highly entertaining.

"Stirring the pot."

I've invented all kinds of good things. I'm probably best known for "Gotyas"—underwater devices for catching Pacific cod. They are a permeable wall—fish can swim one way into a pot but they can't get back out. Gotyas are made of alternating fingers. Some are weighted, some are floating. It has to do with specific gravity versus gravity in a liquid medium. It works like nothing else. But being a fisherman trying to sell them to other fishermen doesn't work too well. These guys who use my gear don't want other guys to know how they're catching the fish, so they swear me to secrecy with confidentiality statements. It's sort of the opposite of advertising, so it makes it difficult to get the word out.

I've worked with a guy, helping him refine square rope. There's more surface area to it so it grips better. But in the textile industry American labor is too expensive, and everyone wants to own the goose that laid the golden egg. If we want to buy their material, they want to buy our idea, so it's complicated. Back in college I did work with explosive metallurgy—mold formation using explosives in water. I got all the way to my thesis and then got kicked out of school for using explosives on state property. It was a catch-22—I couldn't get my degree unless I demonstrated my method, but demonstrating my method got me kicked out. So I never did get my degree.

All this time I fished off and on. My dad was a fisherman during World War II. He told me that if he hadn't spent so much time on whiskey, horses, and women that he'd have been a wealthy man. He fished for sardines and sharks. All they kept of the sharks was the livers—in 5-gallon cans. They made some kind of drugs out of it for the troops.

Even on an Alaska dock, Capt. Larry is immediately identifiable: Just look for the Hawaiian shirt.

It wasn't till early 2000 that I was fishing full-time. I always had the boat. It had been my dad's. A lot of times Kenny *[Hendricks, Larry's cousin, engineer, lifelong best friend, and relief skipper]* ran the boat, and I'd come back for key seasons. I've become sort of the youngest godfather of the fleet, so the *Deadliest Catch* people came to me for information. I was childhood friends with Phil—he's Americana at its best. Sig's father was in this business from its inception, and Sig's a character in himself. I love to get Sig to argue just to rile him up.

Fishermen are really good at talking about something they know nothing about. My forte is stirring the pot. I love to mince words with these guys. Pretty soon I'm talking about how we made cheese on the moon, and they have no idea how we got on that subject or what we're talking about. I use old age and treachery to outfox youth and skill.

Anyway this consulting thing is really a pretty easy job. You just listen to what the producers want to do, tell 'em when what they want to do is impossible, and then figure out a way to do it. If you could tell the way a woman or a fish thinks, you'd be a wealthy man.

A lot of fishermen don't think the way normal people do. Fishing is a world where you navigate by colors, direction, common sense, mathematical tables. We've got uncommon sense and brilliance of mind but we're not always word people. We can be hard to follow. It doesn't translate too well.

"You feel incredibly alive."

I used to fish for the money. After awhile it was because I couldn't stand the thought of sitting behind a desk. Fishing is playing a game as a captain against the rest of the captains. The more information you have, the more it rejuvenates you. You don't even think about fatigue. I can get eight hours of sleep in two hours. I sleep fast. You get used to sleeping fast. I sleep so hard, the heat literally pours off my body. The longest I generally sleep on the boat is three hours. There's the excitement of getting back on the water, the challenge of running the boat. The weather, the current, the beauty of Mother Nature—it's ever-changing at sea. Nothing ever seems the same. Even if you go to some of the same places, the weather, the wildlife, the waterfalls, the landslides—it's all different.

When the season begins, the game comes back to you. You're always thinking ahead, like a chess player. You're thinking about your next move four to five moves out. You're thinking into the future, you don't relive the past. That's what some guys do when they get to the bar afterwards. Three times the total crab catch is caught in the bar because no one wants to admit to being low boat.

But when you're running a boat, you make a decision and it's gone. It's the continuous present. It makes you feel incredibly alive. You have to put all your attention on what you're doing. If you miss a moment you can get thrown off track and make a mistake. It's like driving a race car and you're trying to win the race.

Last week I was in a NASCAR race car. They took me for a few fast laps around the track. They asked me what I thought of it. I said, "It's just like on a boat—the car maneuvers, your body shifts. It's a little bit higher speed." But just like in a boat, you're always watching around you. Crab boat skippers have eyes in the back of their head. We've got senses that have developed different than most people. You gotta be able to see a wave coming, and they come in clumps. Or you'll get a rogue wave. You're always prepared for the unexpected. I'm a slow driver in a car for that reason. I don't speed. I've never hit anything. I hate music on while I drive. People yell at me to speed up.

Same with the boat. Some guys go full speed right off of the dock. Well, their engines burn up. We don't run that hard unless we have to. Our lives are very much dependent on how we treat the boat. Being owner and master I need to bring my crew back safely. *Sea Star* was built in '69. It's in brand-new condition. A steel vessel doesn't degenerate if you keep paint on the surface and fix things as they come along. That costs a lot of money. We spend $300,000 in maintenance for every million dollars we gross. You can get by cheaper, but we don't. If one piston in the main engine goes, we replace them all. The cost multiplies when you do things right.

"Get us more pumps!"

Even so, things can happen. When they did the very first *Deadliest Catch* show, the day before the season started and they started filming, we were sinking and we were ordered by the Coast Guard to evacuate. The boat got this little hole in the lazarette lid *[the lazarette is the compartment farthest back in the boat]*, and somehow the alarm got sheared off, and it filled up with water, and we never knew it. The stern starts going down, but we've got a load of pots on so it takes us a while to get to it. Pretty soon we got enough pots moved and we pop the lazarette lid, and the tail end of the boat is three-fourths full of water. After the water that came through the lid got deep enough in there, stuff started sloshing around and broke a pipe to a seacock *[a valve that lets seawater in]*. So now we're really taking on water.

The Coast Guard shows up and drops one pump to us, then two pumps, but the pumps aren't capable of keeping up, and we're slowly sinking. They ordered us to evacuate. I said, "To hell with that—get us more pumps!" I'd just put close to $500,000 into repairs and maintenance and upgrades to the boat and I'd forgotten to get additional insurance on the extra value, so I wanted to save the boat. Plus we got a fishing season starting the next day.

I kept giving the boat more power so the force of the water against the hull would keep us afloat, and they finally dropped us a couple more pumps, and with all four of them going, we got the boat stabilized to where we could stop the water from going in.

But now we've lost all our steering, because all the electronics for the steering are back there and they don't work too well in saltwater, so we're steering the boat back to Dutch Harbor by hand.

So we get into town and we take all the mess that's in there out and

66

replace the electronics, do some quick wiring, and 12 hours later we're getting our tank inspection, and now I got the film crew on. Well, no one tells them that we were sinking the day before. On the way out the weather's starting to build, and there's a boat giving a mayday, and they finally ask me what that commotion was yesterday. I tell them that we were out there floating around sinking, that we managed to save the boat but that we had to just do the bare minimum to the electronics. These guys are scared spitless. They're saying, "What do you mean, 'The boat was *sinking?'* " Those guys won't *ever* forget that.

The Hometown Boy
Lenny Lekanoff, F/V **Wizard**

*When you talk about those with deep roots in the Alaskan fisheries,
there are many contenders. Several* Deadliest Catch *fishing families
trace Alaskan fishing back two, three, even four generations.*

*But when it comes to who has the most Bering Sea saltwater in
his veins, there's no contention: It's Lenny Lekanoff, by a margin of
several thousand years.*

*Lenny is a native Aleutian Islander whose people have been
pulling sustenance from the Bering Sea since before the dawn of
recorded time. Yet in his 40-some-year lifetime, Lenny has seen
more change come to his native Unalaska Island than have any of
his forebears.*

*He can remember when what's now called Dutch Harbor was a
village of a few hundred people—long before the fishermen and their
big boats and even bigger floating canneries arrived. He's seen the
rise of the fishery and the tremendous cultural and economic changes
that have come with it.*

Wizard*'s engineer is a compact, powerfully built but remarkably
soft-spoken man—quiet, easygoing—in fact downright shy. There's
not a trace of bluster about him. Even when relating life-and-death
struggles with the sea, there's a certain calm in his voice and
demeanor that reflects his long acquaintance with the subject. The
violence of the wind and water have been simple, accepted, even
unremarkable facts of life for generations of Lekanoffs. To Lenny
there's nothing extraordinary about his life or his occupation, save
that it bridges two worlds—and by choice.*

*Lenny lives in Olympia, Washington, with his wife, a lower-48
gal, and his teenage daughter. He's just moved into a new house, and
his claim on the American dream has been well-established for quite
some time. He can't imagine living year-round in Unalaska now,
though he takes his daughter there for a two-week vacation every*

summer and works out of that port during crab seasons. Nor can he imagine ever giving up his tie to the sea.

Tearing down and rebuilding a damaged deck crane aboard Wizard, *Lenny wields open-end wrenches as large as dinosaur femurs with grace and skill. With nary a curse nor a grunt, he methodically reduces the crane's damaged and stubbornly jammed transmission to a neatly arrayed pile of bolts, gears, bearings, and pinions, carefully wiping and inspecting each part for the smallest of flaws. Working on the crane here, in the sunny Seattle docks, is a vacation compared with trying to fix it in the freezing hell of the Bering Sea, and he appreciates that here he can take his time and do a thorough job.*

The relaxed, thoughtful pace of his work reflects in his conversation as he talks about growing up and fishing in the remote Bering Sea.

I can remember being 5, 6, 7 years old in Dutch Harbor when there were 200 to 300 people living there year-round. The first cannery that came in was a floater-processor, a real small one that arrived in the mid-60s.

There were very few boats fishing king crab then. I've seen it go from little 58-foot boats to today—to boats 155 feet long, like *Wizard*. Now the population is, what, 5,500 year-round? When everybody's in town I bet it's 6,000, 7,000. There are three huge canneries there, each with over a thousand employees. You've eaten a McDonald's Filet-O-Fish? They make that fish patty, in its entirety, right in Dutch.

It went from a little tiny hamlet to a booming, bustling, busy little town. We didn't even have a high school until 1972—you had to fly off-island to graduate. We got our first phone service in 1970. We didn't get TV until 1973. The first time I saw a TV I was 12, 13 years old. I never left Dutch until I was 14. I never saw the outside world until then. It was pretty eye-opening.

I have five brothers and four sisters, and I'm the only one who went abroad. They all like it *[in Dutch Harbor]*. I don't like it. There's nothing to do there. Wintertime, it's miserable. I mean it's miserable

As *Wizard's* engineer, Lenny's responsibility is to make sure that the boat's mechanical systems are in top shape. Here he's overhauling the boat's crane.

going fishing, but we do it because that's what we do. But to live there?

He seems genuinely incredulous that anyone would choose to do such a thing.

My wife's from down here, and she does not like it up there. We visit once every 10 years, and that's it. But I take my daughter up there every summer for vacation, and she loves it. If she could move, live up there right now, she would.

I tell her, "Well, we're only here a week or two weeks. Can you imagine living here for six months in the miserable cold?" But she claims she would like it still. She already knows she wants to go to college, but she might want to live up there after she is done.

I ask her, "Why? What would you do?"

She says, "I don't know. My aunts and uncles live here. Why can't I?"

Once you're out of college, you can do what you want, I guess, but fishing is what I've always done.

Monte Colburn, Lenny Lekanoff, and Keith Colburn take a break during dockside preparations to take *Wizard* back to sea.

It started when I was a kid. We'd go beach fishing, subsistence fishing for our own food. As you get older you go out on the skiff, you learn to fish from a boat. First, little skiffs—12-foot, 20-foot boats. As you get older you hear of other kids making money commercially fishing in the summertime. So you somehow find a way of getting onto bigger boats: 38-foot, 48-foot, whatever. You know, you come up fishing. You get involved as you're growing up, you learn. You halibut-fish with other people in the summertime when you're not going to school. Just being in the fishing town, you go with the flow. It's natural.

After high school I did various land jobs, but my older brothers used to fish, and they helped me find a job on a boat. The first big boat I worked on was 98 feet. It was owned by a local native. He gave us all jobs. I've worked on several other boats since then.

I got picked to be the engineer because they saw I could handle it. You know, the boat's got to run. You live on it, it supports you. There's a lot more going on down there than people think. There are a total of four engines: one main engine for propulsion and two or three generators, which also push the hydraulics. Plus the bow thruster—that makes five engines.

The bow thruster is a big propeller in a tunnel in the front of the boat. It pushes the bow of the boat sideways. It's basically just for docking and mooring. Being a single-screw *[one propeller]* boat it doesn't really maneuver very well, as big as it is. It's kind of a tank, really. So the thruster is nice, and as with anything, generally it works most of the time. There's never a shortage of things to fix on a boat.

Your life depends on the engine when you leave the dock, so you've got to get good, clean fuel. You're constantly transferring fuel between tanks to keep the boat balanced as you burn fuel and take on or drop gear. And you want that engine running perfectly all the time. We've never had an engine problem on this boat. That's Keith's doing. He believes in proper maintenance.

After my daughter saw *Deadliest Catch* for the first time, she wanted me to change careers. She said, "It's too dangerous, Dad. You're going to get another job." But fishing is all I know, it's all I've ever done. The money is good, and it keeps you coming back.

But there's more to it than that, I guess. Being born and raised around the water, I like it. I always have an itch. I've just got to go, to be out on the water.

The All-Purpose Outfielder
Monte Colburn, F/V Wizard

There's a clear family resemblance between the Colburn brothers. Monte, a year younger than Keith, shares his brother's stocky build and garrulous nature.

Monte's engine timing is set back a degree or two, though. He's just a tad less intense, less driven than his brother. More easygoing. Listeners don't find themselves on the edge of their chairs quite as much, and tend to sit back, relax, and enjoy Monte's incredibly well-rounded perceptions of the fishing industry from a guy who seems to be comfortable doing just about anything there is to do on a boat—and to enjoy himself immensely in the process.

Monte started fishing a season later than Keith did but remains just as devoted to his calling as his brother. He's served as deckhand, engineer, deck boss, relief skipper, and skipper on a number of boats. Currently he's Keith's relief skipper on Wizard, and the deck boss when he's not up in the house.

The most curious thing about Monte is his ill-fitting nickname. Almost no one calls him by his first name.

"Mouse?" Keith will ask, "What season was that when we were fishing in the Pribilofs and had that storm?" Or "Lenny, while you tear down the crane, Mouse'll be getting in supplies."

"I've been called that since I was a little kid," Monte says with a grin. "Monte Mouse. That was me. I was just a timid little kid, and it stuck."

Initially he was a bit uncertain about owning up to such a nickname when he entered the crab fishery: the land of the tough and the home of the blustery.

"When I first started on this one boat, the engineer said, 'What's your nickname?' I told him I didn't have one."

"He said, 'Everybody's got a nickname—what's yours?' "

"I still wouldn't tell him. It bugged him for days. Finally he said, 'I bet it's a rodent.' "

"I was amazed how close he was coming, but I still wouldn't tell him. Then he started calling me 'Weasel.' Nothing but 'Weasel.' Eventually I decided I might as well tell him, and have my old name back. Now everybody calls me Mouse."

"Eighteen-hour days."

Wizard has been really, really successful over the years due to its size and, of course, to my brother. He's a great fisherman. He's taken a lot of chances on where he's decided to fish, and it's paid off really well.

He and I rotate. He drives 18 hours a day and I drive the other six, and then I'll spend 12 hours outside. So it's basically an 18-hour day for both of us, for the whole crew for that matter.

When I'm outside, I'm a deckhand, just like everybody else. Twelve hours outside isn't too bad. That goes by pretty quick. But you're still working outside, you're still wet, you're still tired. It's a lot different than sitting upstairs for 18 hours out of every day. That in itself, that can be a little bit of a task. Everybody wants to be the skipper until the weather gets bad, or the tough decisions that need to be made come up. And there's always plenty of those.

That's reflected in the pay. For a deckhand, a good year would be $75,000 or $80,000 dollars, maybe even more than that depending on how much you catch. And the skipper is probably going to make $120,000 to $140,000, something like that.

I think a lot of people have the impression that everybody that goes out is a millionaire. It's not true. It's a very good living and you get a lot of time off, but it's not astronomical wages. You can do it for 30 years if your body holds up, but you're only going to end up with what you manage to hang on to. If you go work for the county for 30 years, you're going to walk away with a substantial retirement. There's no retirement plan here.

And unfortunately, a crew member is kind of like a spark plug. You get one that's not working right, you pull it out and you put in a new one. That's the nature of the business. To be competitive, to be efficient, to be safe, you need good people. I've had some great crews over the years and I've had some marginal ones. And even a crew with three good guys and two so-so guys is marginal. Because the three good guys are only capable of so much. It takes a good *group* of guys. And in order to keep good guys around, you've got to pay them good money. As the captain, you're better off taking a little hit yourself and passing it around the crew in order to keep those good guys that you need.

But if someone has to leave or someone gets hurt, you have to find a crewman. There are really not a lot of options. You could fly

Monte exits *Wizard's* wheelhouse. As relief skipper, he drives the boat while his brother Keith is off duty.

somebody in, but that might take a day or two days to get somebody out of the city, and he might end up being a turd anyway. Or you just go into the bar and you look for anyone that's looking for a job. You just grab a guy and hope that he works out. But the pickings are usually pretty thin. Very few success stories come out of people hired in the bar. Hey, if they don't have a job and they're in Dutch Harbor, there's usually a reason. They've got some kind of issue.

Usually they're all real hungry at first, but you'll know within a day or two if they've got what it takes to put up with the hours and the weather, and just the lifestyle itself. A lot of the younger guys can be too young—18, 19, 20 years old. Their moms are still doing their laundry.

At the same time, you don't want to train somebody that's 30 years old, either. Because by the time he has a good grasp on fishing, he's been doing it four or five years. That's about what it takes. Now he's 35, and it's kind of like hiring a quarterback that's 28. It's a young man's game. I'm 43 years old, and I'm fortunate that I'm still physically able to do it. Many people my age can't.

In the past, when we'd go out king crab fishing in a four-day fishery, a seven-day fishery, whatever it was, if you could catch 100,000 pounds, that was the brass ring. 100,000 pounds at five bucks a pound—that's a half-million dollars. Well, that's a quick 30,000 bucks to a crewman—in four days. That's pretty darn good! But you don't get those four days every month, or even twice a year. It's a one-shot deal, and there's just as much a chance you're going to go out and catch 30,000 pounds and the guy's only going to make $7,000. That's where the skipper's stress comes in, because if you've got six crewmen, you've got about 20 or 30 mouths to feed with their wives and kids and everything. There are a lot of people counting on that gear hitting the water at the right spot.

Most guys go to where they've had success before. But crab are really hard to nail down. We call them ghost crab because you think you're on them. Dream on—you're not even close. They run off.

We'll be on big fishing one day, and the next day we get nothing. They either go off the bite and quit feeding, or they go on the march—they just up and run.

There's some neat footage taken by a camera that was set in a pot. It showed the pot hitting the bottom and there were plenty of crab around, but none would go in. Then one or two would enter the pot, and as soon as they started on the bait, it was a frenzy! Hundreds of crabs were fighting to get in! They *all* get in there and they're pounding on the bait, hitting the bait real hard. Then all of a sudden they'd stop and go in the corners and hang out. Then one would go up and start chewing, and they'd all go after it again.

King crab can move pretty fast. They will run. King crab will travel five, six, seven miles in a day. As soon as you think you've got them corralled, they take off, because they forage. They have to travel to find food. They're cleaning the bottom of the ocean.

These days, I think we're taking about 16 or 17 percent of the legal males. That's about our threshold for what we are allocated. It's not a lot. We've seen an awful lot of crab out there. We set pots for 50 miles and saw five or six hundred per pot for opilios—for 60 miles! Holy cow, they were everywhere! They're starting to pile up a little bit down there, and hopefully they'll let us take a little bit more of them. It's hard to say. There's more politics in fishing now than anything. With all the regulations and the quota system, there's more to it than just putting the pots on the boat, grabbing a good group of guys, and going out and going fishing like it used to be.

The Old Salt

Kenny Hendricks, F/V **Sea Star**

Kenny Hendricks is the oldest crewman to appear on Deadliest Catch. *He's about 60—an amazing age in a profession where, as Sig Hansen says, 35 to 40 is considered old. Furthermore Kenny is the very icon of the wizened seaman: With his snow-white beard, twinkling eyes, weathered face, and rail-thin physique, he looks like he could just as well have swung down from a yardarm of a square-rigged clipper as the deck of a modern crabber.*

You can generally find Kenny in the vicinity of Larry Hendricks, and for good reason: The two men are in Kenny's words "cousins that were raised as brothers." Kenny is Larry's relief skipper aboard Sea Star, *and they've been fishing as a team as far back as either can remember.*

They're an Odd Couple *pair, making opposite first impressions: Larry is a disheveled extrovert, a big bear of a man, a careless dresser who can talk about several subjects simultaneously without stopping. Kenny is quiet and slight of build. He speaks slowly, with a deep drawl that's so distinctive, he's instantly identifiable—even over a static-filled marine radio. He generally pipes up when Larry has momentarily run out of breath or exhausted his subject. Kenny then interjects a comment or anecdote. These are always worth hearing and often hilarious—the more so for Kenny's slow, deliberate deadpan. In the dramatic dialogue that chronicles life and times aboard* Sea Star, *Larry may be the main character, but Kenny is the Greek chorus, the voice in the background whose occasional comments prove exceptionally keen.*

The men seem to have opposite thermostats as well: On a day that sees Larry sweating in his unbuttoned Hawaiian shirt, Kenny is neatly bundled in a zipped-up fleece-lined jacket embroidered with Sea Star's *name and logo. He wears new blue jeans, spotless running shoes, and a* Sea Star *cap. His stylish wraparound sunglasses make him look like a cross between the main character in* The Old Man and the Sea *and a 20-something movie star.*

Half the impact of Kenny's stories results from his up-from-the-boots baritone drawl and his impeccable timing, which can turn surprisingly few words into a drama or a joke. For example:

"I started choking once."

Kenny pauses, allowing his listener's imagination to fill in the details of the event.

"So Larry pulls the old Heimlich on me."

Kenny pauses again, giving the "swat a fly with a sledgehammer" image a chance to sink in. Then comes the punch line:

"Well yeah, I quit choking. But now I've got two broken ribs!"

"Not the brightest bulb in the garden."

We're tied up at the docks in Ketchikan once, and this kid comes over and asks to borrow the water hose. He's not the brightest bulb in the flower garden. We give it to him, and he sets it up to fill the water tanks on his boat, then comes over and starts drinking beer with us. Well, his boat's being worked on. They got it all opened up belowdecks. No separate watertight compartments. We walk over Monday morning, and his tanks have overflowed into the rest of the boat, and the boat sank right there at the dock. Kid never turned the water off and filled the boat up. Only Bering Sea crab boat that I know of that sank in freshwater in a dead calm.

Kenny pauses, then delivers the kicker:

Kid blamed us for givin' him the hose.

"All foo-fooed up."

One time this same kid, he got paid and wanted to get all duded up and go into the Elbow Room and pick up girls. So he got some brand-new cowboy boots and a pair of brand-new 501 Jeans. Shrink to fit.

He was working on our boat then, so I tell him I'll wash his jeans for him. He's in a hurry to get to the bar and he thanks me for savin' him some time.

So while he's showerin', I'm washing his jeans, only I tie knots in the legs, one in each leg. Then I washed 'em in hot water. Then I reefed those knots real tight with the deck crane. Then I put 'em in the dryer. By the time I was done there was no way those knots were comin' loose. They were hard as baseballs.

Well, he's still in there getting all foo-fooed up to go into town when I was done, so I told him I'd see him at the bar and that his jeans were in the dryer.

[Pause.]

So he shows up at the bar wearing cutoff Levi's and cowboy boots and lookin' ridiculous, and he was mad as hell.

"My hat won't come off!"

Another time we were at the dock working on the boat. He was messing with me—he did something to me I can't remember and took off running. I was chasing him, and his hat fell off, so I quit chasing him but I got his hat.

He says, "I want my hat."

I said, "Screw you, I'm not giving you your hat."

At least not yet, I wasn't. We were in port and I was painting the inside of the bait freezer with epoxy paint when I get an idea. This paint's got stickum in it, so I get the brush nice and full of this epoxy paint and I run it around the inside of the brim of his hat and I set it there and go off and do something else.

So he sees it, and snatches it, and puts it on his head, and says, "I got my hat back, ha ha!"

I said, "Yep, you sure did."

A few minutes later he feels something funny. Pretty soon gray paint's running out from under the hatband. He can't figure out what's wrong. I can barely contain myself.

He swipes his brow with the back of his hand and looks at it and says, "Oh my God, I'm sweating gray now!"

I almost fell off the boat.

83

Then he says, "Son of a bitch! My hat won't come off! It hurts! Oh, it burns!"

He was ready to kill me when he figured it out.

He was mostly bald with just a little hair on the side of his head to begin with. He had to pretty near shave his head to get that paint off, but he doesn't do a very good job. So he goes to the bar that night with big bald spots and gray paint on his head, and tufts of hair sticking out the back. He was trying to pick up girls, and it wasn't workin'. He couldn't figure out why, and he was such a big guy, no one wanted to tell him and make him mad.

[Despite his size, Kenny has a earned a tough-guy reputation. "Dynamite comes in small packages," he shrugs. Yet he is well-known for fainting at the sight of blood. The first time it happened he was in First Aid training at the University of Washington. Here's how Larry remembers it: "The lights go off, and they're showing us a film with contusions, concussions, amputations, death, the 20 most gruesome pictures you'll ever see. When the lights flipped back on, there were only two of us in the class that were conscious. Kenny's sitting beside me; he's out cold, white as a sheet. I had to treat him for shock."

But that's not what got Kenny known throughout the fleet as a fainter.]

The engineer lopped off his finger some way. I was running the boat and I looked at it and passed out. So the engineer has to treat himself and then treat me too because I was unconscious. He ended up having to talk to the Coast Guard about it himself.

It took a while to live that one down, since everyone heard about it on the radio. They're saying, "What are you going comatose for—he's the one that lost his finger!"

Waaaall, *[he drawls,]* That's the way it was. True story.

Then once when we were fishing, and a pot fell down and hit me on the head and knocked me out cold on the deck. Well Larry comes down out of the wheelhouse to check on me and tells a deckhand to run in and get the smelling salts. Before the deckhand gets back, a wave comes over the deck, and all that freezing-cold water wakes me up. Next thing I know, here's this kid running up with a salt shaker. I say, "Smelling salts, you dumb ass, not table salt!"

[What with all the rigors of his occupation, one wonders whether Kenny's ever considered getting a job ashore.]

I tried it, but it don't work. I went to work for the post office for a little while. Now I met a lot of nice people working at the post office, and for some reason or another they like it and they do it. But I was always getting in trouble. They'd say it was time to take a coffee break. I'd say, "In two minutes we'll be done here. Let's finish up." But no, we gotta take a coffee break. So I wouldn't take a break. I'd keep working and I got in trouble. Then later I'd want a break and I'd take my own break and I got in trouble for that too. It was real easy to figure out that it wasn't going to work for me.

The Kid
Jake Harris, F/V Cornelia Marie

Jake Harris lives a few blocks from his brother Josh. From the outside the house looks similar to Josh's. Inside it couldn't be more different: Oriental rugs, handmade furniture, an easel, paintings in progress, art on the walls. All is immaculate, as though propped for a magazine photo shoot.

None of these refined accoutrements is Jake's. He rents a room here from a friend of his father; the only piece of furniture Jake owns is his bed, recently retrieved from storage. He's often at sea for pretty near a year straight and has no need of a shoreside address.

The dissimilarities between Jake and Josh are striking. Josh is all sharp edges, complete with a mischievous glint in his eye. When he shows up, people know it. Even without saying anything he seems to trumpet his presence.

Jake by comparison seems softer, more indirect—shy in fact. He's dressed nearly identically to his brother, in a T-shirt and cap, but he wears the cap backward. Where Josh is lanky, Jake is downright slight at all of 120 pounds. His voice is quiet, easygoing, matter-of-fact. There's very little drama about him.

It's initially hard to believe that he's "the man"—Captain Phil's heir apparent and Josh's hero and tutor. But even ashore Josh defers to him. And his factual and understated accounts have a drama and power all their own.

"The tar scared out of me."

I was always "the kid" out on the boats. My first time in Alaska I was 7 or 8 years old, gillnetting with my grandfather, picking fish out of a salmon net. When I graduated from high school, I started crabbing. I was 18. You don't see too many people start that young, but I was always planning on crabbing. I figured I would be a fisherman. You make a little bit of money, you start enjoying what you're doing. I was kind of stuck with it.

I like going up there. Even though you never really leave work, and it puts your body through hell, and you're miserable—you're cold, you're wet, you're tired—every season comes to an end. And when it's all over you get to go home and do whatever you want and you have the money to do it. There's a great sense of freedom that comes with it.

My dad was always crab fishing, and I always told him I was going crab fishing. My dad's a tough guy, and he didn't know whether I could physically even do it. So when I graduated from high school, I had to step up or go home. I got the tar scared out of me first season. But the last red crab season, I made 16, 17 grand in three days. The money's been treating us all right ever since we started.

A lot of it sits in the bank actually. You don't even get paid for one season until you go for the next, so a lot of times the check sits in the mailbox. On the boat or in the bank is probably the best place for it. Hopefully I'll be smart with my money. I'll buy a house, rent it out, buy another house. By the time I'm 30 I'll own three houses. Buying and selling houses is the best way to become a millionaire. I've been reading all kinds of real estate books.

I like nice cars too. I'd like to get a Range Rover to go camping in. I know I'd just get in trouble if I got a fast car. I already have speeding tickets. Josh likes fast cars, and his driving record shows it too. I tried to buy a crotch rocket once, a really fast road bike. But just before I was going to pick it up, my dad called and asked me what I was up to. I told him, and he said if I continued to want my job I wouldn't buy a street bike. So I didn't. I guess your life expectancy is like 20 days after you buy one of those.

"Everyone is yelling at you."

Your first job on the boat—no matter how old you are, no matter whether you're the captain's son or not—is the greenhorn. That's the job where everyone is yelling at you, because you don't know what to do, you've never done any of this before. You stay really busy, you start sweating a lot. Your job is to cut up the bait and bait the pots. It's one of the most important jobs on the boat and one of the hardest. If you survive you know you can move up in the crew and eventually get full shares.

Before you go out, the guys try to tell you exactly what's going on so when the boat is rocking around, and there's crab all over the table, and someone's yelling in your ear, you'll know what to do. You try to prepare, you know the knots in advance, but you really learn right there. I've been around those guys since I was a little kid, so they all have an uncle or brother appearance to them.

You learn your little tricks. I'm not very big so I've got to use the sway of the boat to my advantage. You've got to work with all the elements. If you're moving a pot, when the boat takes a roll, put leverage into it. Certain corners of the pot you can tug on to make it go easier. It's all about being smart with what you're grabbing at. A

Jake is by far the smallest of the three Harrises, but he's every bit as tough as his dad, Capt. Phil, center. His older brother Josh, right, calls Jake his hero.

big guy might tire himself out quicker; no matter how big you are, you're not going to be able to push a pot uphill. It's a lot better to use a little trick.

Different seasons you have different issues. Red crab are spiny, so you can rip up your rain gear pretty easy. You go through two or three sets of gear a season or you're soaking wet. Opies you're fishing in January; it freezes, and that's hard on gear too. All seasons combined I probably go through four or five sets of gear a year, plus two or three pair of boots. You put silicone in the holes and patch 'em up; you make 'em last. Even so you spend about $1,500 on gear a year. My dad, he yells at us sometimes about how much money we spend on gear but he's up there in the wheelhouse with the heat on. He's expecting you to go out there in rags. It's way worth it to pay money to buy nice gear and stay a little bit dry.

I like red crab a lot better than opies because there are only two shots of line per pot, 'cause we're fishing in shallower water. The pot comes up faster, so the work is much faster-paced, the crab are a lot bigger—they're big old lumpers, you're hauling 30-dollar bills out of the pots. Opies, you might have over a thousand little crabs in a pot and you've got to sort them all. The weather's nastier, but that makes it a little more exciting. I don't know; opies seem like more of a grind, but it's fun, too, I guess.

"You don't realize just how scary it can get."

My first opie trip the *Big Valley* went down. The season began on the 15th of January, and they had a stack of 218 pots on. The weather was bad, and some boats were staying in, but we decided to take off, and so did *Big Valley.* A couple waves ripped our railings off the port side. Big, steel railings—the water tore them right off.

Two miles away from us, an EPIRB *[Emergency Position-Indicating Radio Beacon, a device that helps rescuers locate crews of ships in trouble]* went off. *Big Valley* had rolled over and gone down. The old man called us off deck and said everyone needs to be looking for survivors. We headed over to the EPIRB's location, going to where the boat should have been on radar. We saw crab totes floating in the water, pot buoys, but no survivors. Six or seven hours later we found our first body. The whole time it's blowing and storming.

That night I saw green water hit the wheelhouse windows. My old man's got a pretty big boat. It's a little scary.

We found some more bodies after that. A Coast Guard helo and a rescue diver flew over and picked 'em off the boat. They finally found one guy alive in a life raft—one guy out of five.

You always hear that it's scary out there but you don't realize just how scary it can get. You get that feeling in your stomach…

[Jake's words trail off, and he's silent for a moment.]

You're kind of wishing you went to college instead, but it just turns out to be another night out there doing your job.

The scary part is when fishermen took a look at *Big Valley* before she left, she had pots stacked five high. That's a little top-heavy. A lot of people said something before the boat left port, and they were right. *Big Valley* got hit by a wave, and the boat rolled over. Too many pots.

[Jake pauses again—another moment of silence for the ill-fated Big Valley *crew.]*

It's cool having a captain that's my dad. He won't put anybody in harm's way. Me and my dad the last four years have really connected. He's more a buddy to me than a dad. It wasn't until I went fishing and entered his world that I really got to know him. Then I figured out why he was always gone, what he did, and we connected a lot more. It's pretty weird but pretty cool to work with my brother and my old man on the boat up there. Not a lot of people can say they do that.

Josh and I lived together until we were about 14, but we didn't get along. We fought. Now it's like he's a really good buddy. His first trip out on the boat, I'd hear all the guys yelling at him. … I made sure he knew exactly what he was doing. I taught him all the tricks that make you faster. He's a good listener, so we worked really well together.

Off the boat we still hang out; a lot of his friends are my friends. We're growing more and more together as we go on.

"The television thing."

It's a lot more crowded with a film crew on the boat. Fishing we've just got five crew and the captain. It's real mellow. With the camera guys we had three extra people. That's three more mouths to feed, three more people to bunk and trip over. The camera guys you can tell are from California. At first they'd leave their dishes on the galley table. I'd throw them in their bunk. They've got to clean up their own mess, just like anyone else on board.

They're always trying to get the really cool shots. They're right next to the pot so you have one eye on them all the time because the boat's rolling around, the pots are untied, and you can get smashed. So you watch over them, especially on deck.

The television thing made life a whole lot different. I'm still kind of taking it all in. Josh likes the camera. I like to do my own things, so the attention is kind of weird for me. When you're in a room full of girls, the TV thing happening is pretty cool. You don't get to see too many girls when you're on the boat, so it's nice to go have fun. But when you're in a grocery store and a bunch of people walk up to you and want to talk—well, the first 10 or 20 times it's pretty cool. But after that, fishing is the last thing on your mind.

It's weird: There we are out there in the middle of nowhere. There's no real life for hundreds of miles around: no streets, cars, stores, nothing. You got the boat, the ocean, the seagulls—and then there are these guys holding up cameras so millions upon millions of people can watch what just happened to you. The whole rock star status *[he shakes his head]* ... I guess a kid could have some fun—I *have* had some fun—but Bering Sea rock stars?

Yeah I get fan mail. A hundred pages a day some days. I've gotten 110 pages of friend requests *[on myspace.com]*. People think it's an exciting way to make a living and they want to meet you and hang out with you. They just want to have fun, I guess.

Mostly when I'm ashore I try to go camping. I do a lot of snowboarding. I'm usually known for breaking my arm, my ribs, my chin, my jaw. I've always been prone to do things that in the long run are not too smart, just to get my heart pumping. I skateboard, I ride the half-pipe, I go wake-boarding. I like to go cliff jumping—there's this one place where you can make a 70-foot dive into the river. There's a rope swing where you can swing out 40 feet. It makes you feel alive.

But I've slowed down a little bit. I like to go bay fishing—crack open a beer and drop a line in the water and see what you catch. Dad used to have a big yacht that we'd cruise around in. I've got a ski boat that I bought from my old man; it's set up for downriggers so I can go out on the sound and go fishing.

No, I never get tired of the water. There's something about it—I like getting wet.

The Greenhorn
Josh Harris, F/V Cornelia Marie

Josh Harris lives in a small town nestled in a valley of the foothills northwest of Seattle. There's a main street, a couple of farm supply stores, a bank or two, a few cafes, a school. In a new development built on what used to be a cow field at the edge of town, roads and houses dot the landscape like a printed circuit. Josh lives in one of these new townhouses—the kind with a short driveway leading to a big garage door with a front door tucked beside it. A pair of little import sport sedans wait in the driveway, each outfitted with wide chrome wheels, gaping exhaust pipes, tinted windows, and body kits.

Inside, mounds of laundry cover the floor of the entry hall and living room beyond. It resembles a house-size version of the jumble of clothing and gear typically seen in the stateroom of a deckhand.

Perhaps for that reason, even ashore Josh prefers the outdoors and talks with friends and visitors in the driveway—on deck, as it were— instead of inside. He lights up a cig, leans on a fender, and says, "So what's happenin', man?" He's as likely to get up at noon or 4 p.m. as at any other time and often has the somewhat hollow-eyed look of someone who has a very active night life.

Josh is clearly a live-for-the-minute kind of guy. School? What was that? He was a party animal. Never made it to graduation and didn't really care. Fate and his father, Captain Phil Harris, landed him a job as Cornelia Marie's greenhorn just as Deadliest Catch cameramen first came aboard.

It was a fortuitous coincidence. Josh's devilish good looks—jet-black hair, neatly trimmed beard, dead-eye Clint-Eastwood-style squint—and extroversion made him an instant favorite on the show. His devil-may-care, life-on-the-edge persona makes a great foil for his father's tough-guy, this-is-serious-business demeanor. The two of them define generational conflict: usually good-natured, sometimes spicy, and always dramatic.

There's no denying that Josh isn't shy and doesn't mind attention—whether he's getting it from the Deadliest Catch *cameras, his father, the rest of the crew, or fans of the show. He has a keen interest in cars, women, and partying. Generally he stands out in a crowd.*

But he can be surprisingly introspective as well. He has a great deal of pride in his family and his fishing roots, a tremendous admiration for his father as a man and a skipper, and a deep love and respect for his younger brother, Jake, who is a Cornelia Marie *deckhand and Josh's shipboard mentor. Josh also gets downright sober when talking about the fearsome power of the Bering Sea and the nightmarish trauma of seeing his first body floating face down after a sinking. He relates it all with an unguarded, here's-the-way-it-is manner that lends authenticity and immediacy to his stories—and proves that you don't have to be a wizened veteran of the Bering Sea to have some pretty amazing tales to tell.*

"I want him to recognize that I'm the man too."

I started fishing with my grandfather and my dad on a gillnetter when I was just a kid to make money for school clothes. When I was 18 I got a job on a dragger. From there I got offered a job on a 300-foot fish-processing ship. It's basically a floating cannery. I worked on what they called the "slime line," gutting and filleting fish. We'd process 120 tons every eight to 12 hours. Fishing boats are constantly coming up to us and off-loading. They're bringing up a net that's a football field long, 9½ feet wide and 10 feet tall full of pollack.

Engineering paid a lot better than gutting fish, so after working 16 hours a day I'd volunteer to help the engineer for a couple hours after my shift was over. I'd change the oil in the generators, do whatever he needed me to. He ended up getting cancer, and I was promoted to oiler. I almost didn't survive that job. A Cat generator almost ate me alive.

After I got that injury, I took some time off. My girl at the time didn't want me to go fishing, so I started working sandblasting and

At sea or ashore, Jake and Josh can generally be found together, sharing a chore, enjoying a laugh—or both.

painting water towers. Heights are a scary mother. The pay was OK, but you could only work when it wasn't raining, which around here is only about half the time.

Then I got a phone call from my father *[Captain Phil Harris of Cornelia Marie]* asking if I'd like to come work on the boat year-round. He said, "This is your opportunity to shine. It's red crab, it's pretty easy. If you do good you can continue to work on my boat. I really don't expect you to make it, but I'm giving you a shot."

I was always trying to prove a point with my younger brother. Jake is my hero. I want him to recognize that I'm the man too—that I could do it. I wanted to prove to myself I could do it. Finally I wanted to prove to my family I could do it. I have respect for my family. It's a fishing family from my grandfather on, and I wanted to show them that I had it in my blood. So in 2000 I did my first red crab season.

"I'm never coming out here again!"

It was pretty wild. We were working in hundred-mile-an-hour winds
and 50-plus-foot waves. One of our fishing partners took a wave
through the wheelhouse that blew out all the windows.

There's nothing like seeing a 200-foot-long boat right next to you,
all lit up like day with these huge halogen lights, seem to rise up like
a UFO, but it's just a wave taking it up. It hangs there for a moment.
Then it just completely disappears. Everything turns black. It just
drops out of sight. That's how big the waves were. And when we fell
off the backsides of the waves it felt like free-fall—like you're just
dropping through the air like there's nothing underneath you. And
I'm thinking, "This is some serious stuff. This is nuts." I didn't say
anything, being the new guy, but one of the old deckhands looked at
me and said, "Yeah, this is some serious stuff, but it's what we do, so
get used to it." I thought, "This is crazy. I'm never coming out here
again!" But I made it through red crab season. And the money!
In three days—two days and 11 hours to be exact—I earned a big slug
of cash. So I came back.

My job as greenhorn was to crawl in the pot after it had been pulled
up and dumped, get the old bait unhooked, hook on the new bait, make
sure there were no crabs in there, and then get the hell out as fast as I
can. On our boat the pot's not fastened down when I'm in there. You
take a good wave, that pot can shoot right off the boat. You can go for
a swim. Or you get slammed into something on deck while you're in
the pot. That ain't great either. But my dad knows how to take care of
his crew. He usually sets it up so that if anything happens, you'll get
blown onto the deck rather than overboard.

And I do mean blown. The power of Mother Nature is immense,
man. It'll blow a pot off the deck like you'd blow a candle out.
The sound of the wind in the rigging is like the stuff you'd hear
in the scariest movie. It just shrieks and howls. That stuff's scary.
The power that those waves possess—you see them on TV, but
they're bigger in real life. The wind is blowing birds right out of

the sky. You're sitting in waves as big as buildings. It's your worst nightmare. The waves hit the boat so hard, it bends steel. It will contort it like you wouldn't believe. Thousands of gallons of raw energy, you can't even fathom it. Nobody's supposed to be out there. Humans aren't meant for that environment. You just hope to make it through another day.

"Dance, puppet!"

Crab fishing is definitely a rough sport. You do whatever they tell you to do out there because they're telling you so you can stay alive. You're like a puppet—they put you out there and it's, "Dance, puppet!" And you dance.

It's a moving environment. The simplest stuff can be impossible to do. Try to make an espresso in 50-foot waves. Now try baiting a pot. There's a lot of learning involved. Even before you go out there you've got to mentally prepare. Nobody wants to do bait so you're generally stuck doing it until somebody quits.

Flooding, fires, deaths, serious injury, men overboard … screwed-up stuff happens out there. You're not near anybody, people are hundreds of miles away. You have a bad day out there, someone goes home in a body bag or gets seriously injured. You wake up to start your watch and think, "What am I doing out here? Did that really happen last night?"

Once I was sitting at a restaurant and this lady was saying to her husband, "God, I hate work, I had a rough day." She was a salesperson. I just stopped eating and stared at her, and she kept going on about what a terrible day she'd had. Eventually they noticed me. They recognized me right away and started looking down at their plates. They got real quiet. I said, "Yeah, I have those days too. They're a little bit different." That kind of put things in perspective for her. They thanked me and told me that they really liked the show.

I've survived so far because I learned from the best. My initiation was working with Roger Jensen. He's the hardest-core mother that ever stepped foot on the Bering Sea. He'd say stuff like, "Wouldn't it be cool if we never had to sleep?" And he'd mean it! He taught me how to start fishing.

"They were calling me Purple. "

But he'd prank me, too. One time he tells me: "Climb in this crab brailer."

A crab brailer is a big, circular basket that folds up as it hits the ground. We use it to unload the boat. So we're in port at the dock, and he says, "Climb in this crab brailer. I'll hoist you up with the deck crane and shake you around a bit." So I hop in, and he lifts me up with the crane, and then I hear my dad on the loud hailer saying, "Drop him over the side!"

So Roger starts lowering me into the water. I'm screaming and yelling, but they just laughed. They slowly lowered me in, right up to my waist. Then they let me sit there and think about the situation. The water was 35 degrees, it's starting to snow, ice is starting to form. They were calling me "purple." I didn't need them to tell me that. I was cold enough to know that my stuff was numb.

"A messed-up fishing family."

On the boat everybody works together as one dysfunctional family. We're all in each others' face 24/7, so we've got to get along. Either that or someone will go for a swim, get a black eye, get fired, or worse. It's a pretty good group of guys. We can all throw our two cents in. But when my dad hops on the hailer and says, "This is what I want done," we just do it. Like a family. A fishing family. A messed-up fishing family.

My dad, we all trust him with our lives. It's a comfortable feeling. If there's anybody that's going to take care of you, it's Dad.

My brother, Jake, is one of the best people for me to work with. He understands me, he understands how to explain things to me really well. If I can count on anybody, it is that kid. He's my best buddy in the world, my roommate on the boat. He doesn't put me down. He says, "Try to do it faster than me, try to do it better than I can." He wants to see me do good, to see me succeed. Jake, there ain't no shame to his game; he put his time in but he'll still cut up cod with me on his time off when he could be taking a nap or getting something to eat. Just to help me out. I look up to him, and watch him, and mimic him because he's really good at what he does. He's just 120 pounds and he's wrestling 700-pound pots better'n some of the big guys. He doesn't bitch and moan, he just works. Rip it and grip it.

That's because crab fishing is 40 percent physical, 60 percent mental. You focus on what's going on at home when you're fishing or you'll go crazy. You remind yourself of the money you're making. This is a great way to get a house and pay it off. I'm 24 years old. I don't know anyone my age who owns a house. It's a way to get a jump on life. I want to be successful, and this will give me the tools I need.

If I can survive.

"Once you get a taste of living on the edge . . ."
Josh is hardly all work and no play, however. He can party as hard as he can fish. He uses the phrase "living on the edge" quite often when describing his recreational pursuits.

My hobby is cars. I love import cars. My last one I had 30 grand into—a motor, crazy flip-flop paint job, a stereo that would blow the shirts off girls. It would keep up with a Viper until sixth gear: 156 miles an hour. Once you get a taste of living on the edge you start looking for it in everything you do. Adrenaline junkies we are. The thrill, it makes you feel alive.

In this business you live every day like it's your last. Fishermen get a bad rep for being party animals and doing bad things, but it's to forget what happened when you were out fishing. There are a lot of lonely nights out there, freezing your ass off, just about dying every night. You never know if you're going to make it back home again. So you never know what's going to happen when you're partying with fishermen. Chicks get on top of the bar and start dancing, and people are looking at you and saying, "Why is he so wild?" It's because we're happy to be alive. We made it back. We're happy just to be here. I don't think that changes. I don't know how Grandpa partied, but I've heard stories about the old man. He wasn't any different than us. He might have been a little wilder actually.

So why do I keep doing it? I used to hate it so much, but you learn to love it. First, it's the paycheck. Slide it under the grate to the teller and she gives you that bug-eyed look when she sees the amount and you're like, "Yeah, I was just up in the Bering Sea kicking ass." Second, some days when you're out there it's really nice weather, and its more like hanging out with your buddies than it is working. Even though you're working your ass off you're getting big numbers in the crab pot. You smell the ocean, it's beautiful. You're off in your own little world, and it's the most beautiful place you could ever be, with the best people you could ever be with.

We have a lot of ha-has on the boat. Me and Jake will team up on my dad. Jake will get me sometimes. We kid about the good times, the old times when we were kids. The three of us together, it is a fun deal. The old man, I think he's proud of us. So it all works out.

"Granted, we're no saints . . ."

The film crews, they definitely add another element. They try to be as respectful as possible and stay out of your way, but they're not fishermen. They're in your face all the time, they ask redundant questions, they get in the way. Sometimes they about get themselves killed. One of the cameramen, Zach, he would work with us. He learned all our routines, and we'd have competitions with him. He never got seasick. He's a wild man. He's crazy. He loves to get a good shot. Once he wanted a big-wave shot, and we're rockin' and rollin', and he's screaming at the ocean, "Is that all you've got?"

Others, they'd get seasick, and we'd call them Ralph. They'd think, "We've gone lobstering, we'll be fine." Well, we're bigger.

We've got bigger boats, bigger pots, bigger waves, bigger problems, bigger everything.

You never really know what you're going to see on the show. It's weird, it's like watching a nightmare that you had a long time ago and you find out that it really happened. Watching it at home, it makes you grab a blanket and curl up a little tighter. You're thinking: "I remember that night. I was cold. My boot leaked. I was soooo tired."

Mostly the show affects us on land. Fan mail—I get like 150 to 700 letters a day. Most of it's done electronically, by email. I try to answer as many as I can. I've gotten some pretty cool letters, like from parents who have kids with cancer who tell me that their 5-year-old son who could go at any time prolongs his life just to stay up to watch the show. You have a chance to make a difference in people's lives. It's a good thing. Granted, we're no saints. We've done a lot of wrong in life. But it's cool that with this show we can do something right.

"We're just fishermen."

Really we're just fishermen. To some people we're more than that, but that's really all we are. I go to the same bar, I eat the same food I always did. Someone came up to us once and said, "You guys are drinking Bud Lite in cans—aren't you a bit above that now?"

Nah. I just want to hang out and chill.

CHAPTER 2

DESPERATE HOURS

The dictionary defines *"desperate" as unbearable, extreme, nearly hopeless, critical. This is how the men of* Deadliest Catch *describe desperate: "I knew I was going to die." "So this is what it's like to die." "I can't make it!"*

All too often for them, "desperate" is on the knife-edge between life and death. Desperation comes in many forms on the Bering Sea: Fire. Ice. A slip of the foot. The cannonlike parting of an overstrained line. Mammoth waves. Sinking boats. The snap of a man's mind as it breaks under pressure.

Consider the description of a single wave, from Captain Keith Colburn: "We started to rise and rise like an elevator that's going to go right through the roof. And as we got onto the crest of that thing, the entire 155 feet of Wizard *was on the face of that wave. The top of it was a good 15 or 20 feet of frothing foam, and we seemed to hang there forever with the water just boiling away from the hull on both sides of the wheelhouse as we were literally surfing down the side of that wave."*

Here is a collection of extreme-but-true tales from those who have been to desperation and back.

WAVES

If **Deadliest Catch** *has a visual theme, it's "Big Waves." A combination of shrieking winds, strong currents, and shallow water makes the Bering Sea a cauldron for combers that are as tall as office buildings and nearly as steep. Such a wave can roll a crab boat over if it catches one "in the trough," or side to the sea. It can simply overwhelm the boat, swallowing it whole. Or it can punch the boat's lights out, breaking the wheelhouse windows and gutting what's inside, knocking out the boat's command center, and leaving it vulnerable to the next wall of water that comes along. All three events are frequently deadly.*

"Here she comes!"
—Captain Sig Hansen

We've been hit by a couple of rogue waves. I've seen the worst ones after a storm. They're double trouble, because that's when you think everything is calm and safe and that you're in the clear.

One time we'd just started to pull gear. I'm at a dead stop, and we've got a line in the block, the guys are pulling a pot on board, and all of a sudden *here she comes*. It peaked up out of nowhere—I mean, *nowhere*—and it engulfed everything.

It wasn't so much the height of this wave—it had a little higher peak than the rest, but not much—but it just had that momentum to it. It had more speed. It was moving so fast, it didn't give the boat a chance to react. Most waves, you'll rise with the wave. This one just buried the boat. I cannot believe that it didn't take the windows out. It went straight over the top of the wheelhouse—solid water.

[If the wave had been taller, Sig probably would have noticed it earlier and been able to get on the loud hailer to warn his crew. But instead he suddenly found himself underwater. If the wave had contained fish, Sig would have been looking them in the eye. Since Northwestern's *pilothouse is on the front of the boat, Sig was actually in more danger at that point than his men were—for a few*

split seconds the boat was running straight into the side of the fast-moving wave, and while the bow and pilothouse were underwater, the deck behind it was still basking in sunshine.

Without time to grab the mike and yell to the crew, Sig reflexively did two things at once—he dove under the boat's dashboard, where he'd be at least somewhat protected if glass began to fly, and at the same time "buttoned down"—slammed his hand down on the pot-launching buzzer and kept it there.]

I'm laying on the buzzer—that's all I can do. The guys know that when they hear a constant buzzer, it means *run!* Something's coming. They run forward right behind the house and hang on.

[The impact of the wave felt as though the boat had dropped, bow down, off a bridge and into the water. Sig slammed into the intersection of the floor and the front wall of the pilothouse, the force of the collision pinning him down. As soon as he could move, he was on his feet, heading for the pilothouse door to check on his crew. In fact he got to the door before the pilothouse fully emerged from the wave. As he opened the door a torrent of green water hit him. Sig barely noticed.]

I'm screaming at the top of my lungs—you know—"Where's my guys?!" And it's pouring down on me, and as I look back at what should be the rest of the boat, it's just water. The boat has disappeared. Except for the pilothouse, every part of the boat is so far underwater, you can't even see it.

Then I can barely see the rails. And then the next thing you know, I can see these heads popping up out of the water that's still covering the deck. And they are laughing at me. They were all the way forward, hanging on. They could hear me screaming so they knew that I was concerned.

["Concerned," of course, is an understatement.]

We got hit with another one—same thing, fishing after a storm. Fishing was great, the crab tanks were full, we were just topping off at the last maybe 15 pots. It was a beautiful, flat calm, just a little lumpy. We're in the ditch, just doing our thing, and the boat was heavy, it was full of crab, and everybody was happy. I was in a great mood and playing music in the wheelhouse—which I never do anymore because of what happened that day. You know you're just in a good mood. You're like, "Hey, we're full; we're going to be first in."

And then another speedy freight train came at us, and when it hit the boat, I felt like I was just a half a second too late hitting the buzzer. By the time I saw it, it was dark *[the wave was so tall, it obscured the sky]*. Brad Parker, our chief engineer who had been on the boat for 19 years, got hit, and it threw him completely across the deck. We thought it killed him. He was lying all hunched up over a tote and he wasn't moving. Fortunately he was conscious and had the sense not to move too quickly after an injury. He ended up chipping something in his spine, but was otherwise OK. So we took him in and got him sent home.

It was so bizarre because it was flat calm. There were no whitecaps. And that's the only incident of serious injury that we have had, knock on wood. And it was flat calm at the time. But that just proves my point about all the variables. If the boat had a little more freeboard at the time—if she had two tanks full rather than three, or if we'd had a little less fuel on board …

You know all these things play into it. I feel guilty because I feel like if I had seen that wave maybe half a second sooner, maybe he could have ducked or something. There were other guys out there. He just happened to be the one to get in the funnel. He's not just crew, he's my friend. Anyway it happened. But as far as major pain or anything, no. He went home, went to the doctor, and then he was right back at it again.

Working in waves that dwarf even the largest boats is almost an everyday event for Bering Sea crab fishermen.

"There wasn't any water on the other side."

—Captain Phil Harris

It was blowing 150, and we were in the biggest seas I've ever seen. They were well over 100 feet. There was a big freighter, a log-hauling ship that got blown off course out there. He's 1,200 or 1,500 feet long and he's taking the bow under. One wave took out these great big I-beams that are 6 feet by 6 feet, and he lost 1,800 logs in one swipe. That skipper was on the radio screaming and yelling that he's going down. You take a 1,500-foot ship and the whole bow is underneath the water—those guys aren't used to that. He's right there among us, freaking out.

We're jogging into it, and we came up on a wave, and we're going up, and up, and up. I'm thinking, "Holy crap!" This one was just huge! We got to the top, and there wasn't any water on the other side, so we free-fell about 100 feet.

When we came down and hit solid water again, it spun us around and snapped one of the rudders right off. And those rudders are huge—8 or 9 feet high, solid steel.

It seemed like every alarm on the boat was going off. Steering's going off. Main alarm is going off. You don't know what the hell's going on. I'm running around trying to hold on and to find out what alarms are going off. The boat isn't steering like it should, and I don't know what the problem is, but it's serious because if you get sideways to the waves, it just rolls you right over, so you want to make sure you're not sideways.

[With only one of two rudders left to steer the 180-foot-long Cornelia Marie *and a boat that had just made an unintentional U-turn, Captain Phil can't take the safest course and jog into the huge waves. The next and only option for survival is to run straight before them and hope he can maintain control of the boat as it surfs down the mountains of water—by no means a certain proposition. But at that point he has no choice.]*

And a friend of mine on the *Siberian Sea* called up and he said,

Aboard a crab boat, "rain gear" is a misnomer: Even on blue-sky days, crews get doused with spray—and sometimes nearly submerged in green water.

"What's it like going before it? What do they look like coming up behind you?"

I'm right at the back door. All I gotta to do is turn around and look out the window. I wouldn't do it. I said, "I can't look. If I do I firmly believe I'll have a heart attack."

"Right down to bare steel."
—Captain Phil Harris

In that same storm was a big oil supply boat that they turned into a crab boat. They're 180 feet long, house forward. The guy's jogging into it, and this wave came and blew right through the front windows, and out the back windows, and blew the back wheelhouse door right off the boat. He's sitting in the chair, and when that happened it blew him, the chair, and everything right out the back door and down two flights of stairs. He was still in the chair, and fortunately he got tangled up in a railing or he would have drowned right there. But it just leveled the inside of the boat. It's the equivalent of taking two sticks of dynamite, putting it in there, and lighting it off: There's nothing left. All the electronics are gone, all the wood is gone. There's no counters left, no walls left, no chart table, no nothing. Everything's right down to bare steel.

"All the guts in his arm were fried."
—Captain Phil Harris

Another guy was resting his arm on the switch panel for the big sodium lights when the wave took his windows out. Well, that mother just lit up like a Christmas tree. And he had 240 volts going through him and he couldn't pull his arm off the switch panel. He's just sitting there like that until the generator shut off. He shorted out the whole generator with his body. Some little boat out of King Cove.

Anyway he's all cut up from the glass but he's alive. And he got the boat situated where they were stable, they aren't going to sink, but in the week following all the flesh fell off his arm until it was just bone. All the guts in his arm were fried by all that power. It was brutal.

"I couldn't turn to help them."
—Captain Phil Harris

There were 15 maydays in about an hour—bang!—the Coast Guard was overwhelmed. So many maydays, so many guys going down. One guy took a wave, and it put the whole boat underwater, and they sank right there in the matter of about a minute. And the guys got in the life raft as the boat is sinking and the generator was still running. When they were in the life raft, they look down and they could see the boat, the sodium lights still on. The boat's 30 feet underwater, going down.

They were right next to me, and I couldn't turn to help them. If I had turned my boat I would have rolled over—boom!—like that.

With "uphill" and "downhill" changing every second, moving an 800-pound crab pot—or keeping it from moving—can be an Olympic-level challenge.

So what do you do? They're in that life raft in 70- or 80-foot seas. Fortunately they survived.

That was the strongest wind I've ever been in. They recorded 225 knots in Akatan. We were about 100 miles away. So I think where we were, the wind was probably between 180 and 200, and the current was running against the wind. That's what makes the seas so high.

"That's a WAVE, man!"
—Captain Corky Tilley

My first rogue wave, we're on *Westward Wind*, a house-aft boat. We'd finished up red crab season and were heading out to the Pribilof Islands to fish blue crab. We had a full load of gear on, so we were heavy. A buddy of mine we call Griz and I are at the chart table looking toward the stern. I notice something funny out the back window so I lean down and see what looks like a huge white light right behind us. It was as high as the moon but it wasn't shaped like the moon. I say, "Griz, what's *that?*"

He looks and says, "That's a *WAVE*, man!"

[What Corky has noticed is the curling top and foaming spray of a huge, fast-moving wave as tall as a towering billboard and nearly as steep. With only seconds before it hits and no time to turn the boat into it, all the two men can do is hang on and pray.]

The wave went completely over the stern. It hit so hard, we were knocked down on our side. *Western Wind* has vent pipes on the stern that go 30 feet up in the air and then turn back down again in a U-shape. We rolled completely over on our port side so far, those pipes filled with water.

[There is no assurance the boat can right itself. The hit is violent, the deck is laden with pots—it is the same scenario that would later roll Big Valley *and send four crewmen to their deaths.]* Western Wind *is prudently loaded and operating within its stability-chart-determined safe range. But no charts are designed to account for a wave of that magnitude, much less predict a boat's chances of recovery from the almost inconceivable event of those three-story-tall vent pipes filling with water.*

The entire wheelhouse crew is thrown violently to the starboard side. Seawater from the flooded vent system pours in everywhere. The boat hangs precariously, the pilothouse floor almost vertical. No one knows whether the list will turn into a roll or whether the heavily laden crabber will right herself.

As the boat lies on its side in the rough seas, seemingly trying to make up its mind whether to fight back upright or turn belly up, the crew struggles to respond. They know that if the vent pipes fill, the engine air intakes are in danger of sucking ocean as well—something that can hydrolock Western Wind*'s big diesel engines, stopping them instantly and permanently. With no power*

As water boils away from the hull as it parts a wave, a crewman prepares to toss a shot of line overboard.

to maneuver, the boat would surely fall victim to the next wave even if it survives this one.

Walt, the skipper, makes his way up to the wheelhouse, crawls over to the helm station, and pulls back on the throttles, reducing the intake suction—and the chance that his engines will choke on seawater and die.

Meanwhile Corky and Griz scramble for the pilothouse stairs and the three-story trip down to the engine room. The huge quantity of water that has filled the big vent pipes now courses through the fresh-air ducts and rains into every room in the house. For a moment, disoriented by the boat's extreme list, the crew can't tell whether they have rolled and are about to drown in their own house or whether the torrent of icy seawater will abate. They don't waste much time wondering. If they are going to drown, they are going to drown. But if

A camera captures a few hundred gallons of airborne water a split-second before it hits the deck.

the boat does come back upright, they need a fully functioning engine room if they are to stay afloat.

As they scramble down the slippery staircase, the men hear the main engines still hammering away. That's the good news. The bad news is that they also hear something else—and that sound could spell disaster.

Short of losing the mains, the second most crippling blow that can happen to a crabber is electrical failure. If the ship's generators go down, steering the ship becomes nearly impossible, especially in heavy weather. And if anything breaks loose in the engine compartment and starts flailing around, it can damage the ship's wiring or other mechanicals, killing power—or worse, starting a fire.

What they hear over the din of the main engines sounds like a demolition derby. When they reach the top of the engine room stairs, they discover why: A four-cylinder diesel generator has broken loose. It skids across the deck plates and crashes into the bulkheads, the main engines, the stairway, whatever it comes up against. The engine ricochets around unpredictably with every surge and toss of the struggling, sea-battered hull.

Looking at where the generator should have been quickly tells Corky and Griz what has happened: When the boat was built a few months previously, a shipyard worker had forgotten to weld the generator to its mounting bed. Until now it has been held in place only by the flimsy clamps on its cooling hoses, which quickly gave way when the wave hit. If Corky and Griz can't figure out how to lasso the half-ton chunk of cast iron, it not only will beat itself to junk—it could destroy the boat from the inside out.

Somehow the two men must tackle and chain down the loose generator without getting themselves crushed.

When asked how, Corky says with a shrug and a grin, "We were motivated."

"Mayday! Mayday!"

We got back to the wheelhouse and we heard a "Mayday! Mayday!" real faint on the radio. We turned up the volume and we heard a voice. It was a crewman of a boat not too far from us that got hit by the same wave. He said he didn't know where he was—all his electronics were out, his generators were out, he couldn't steer the boat, that a huge rogue wave had taken out the spinner window *[a round, motorized window that spins at high speed to keep it clear of rain and ice]* at the helm station, and that the skipper was on the floor turning blue and foaming at the mouth. The crewman said he thought his skipper was having a heart attack.

Walt turned to us and said, "No, that poor bastard isn't having a heart attack. That spinner window came at him and broke his neck." He turned out to be right: That guy ate that big heavy spinner window, and it killed him.

We couldn't move. We jogged into that storm for a day and a half after that. It was rough. We couldn't have gotten to that boat even if we had known where they were. That rogue wave killed the skipper of that boat and nearly killed us. Fortunately the Coast Guard got a cross-fix on that boat and got a cutter out to them. The rest of their crew survived.

"Then there's an explosion."
—Captain Phil Harris

A lot of times a big wave will pick the wheelhouse up and move it back a couple feet. Bust it right off the boat. We've taken waves that blew out the windows on the *Cornelia*. They're three and a half stories above the waterline. I had been sitting in the chair for 50 or 60 hours that time and I was beat. We were just jogging into it. I was talking to Tony, my engineer, who was going to take the wheel watch for a little bit so I could lie down. The weather was coming off the bow quarter, and I said, "Look, you gotta watch for big ones like this," and I pointed to one that was coming.

Often on the Bering Sea, it can be hard to determine where the water ends and the air begins. Crab boat crews work in the slosh and froth that mark the boundary.

That wave came and started kind of dancing. It came right over the boat. First we're blinded by the spray, and then there was an explosion, and it blew these three-quarter-inch Plexiglas bulletproof windows right out of their frames. I hear Tony screaming bloody murder and I didn't know what he was screaming about, 'cause it was just black. But we had taken the three middle windows out. He was sitting on a settee beside me in the wheelhouse. The windows missed me, and he took a direct hit.

That wave probably dumped four or five hundred gallons of water in the wheelhouse. That water ran down into the galley and into the staterooms, and we have to open up the door to let it out. Tony was squealing. I didn't know if he was cut up or what happened. So immediately I put out a mayday—saying, "Hey look, I just took these windows out; we got six souls on board," and giving my position. I don't know what's going to happen next. You don't know whether you've got structural damage or just what. So you give your position, so if other boats are around you, they're aware that you're in trouble—and also to watch out for the rogue wave that got you.

Then I dealt with Tony, made sure he was OK. And then we figure out what we're going to do. We got the boat spun around and put plywood in front of the windows just to keep the water from coming in. And then we try to get to town.

"It rolled the boat completely over."
—Captain Corky Tilley
[Corky's second experience with a rogue wave created some of the most dramatic footage ever shown on Deadliest Catch. *During season 2, episode 14,* Aleutian Ballad *was knocked on its side by a rogue wave. Here's how Corky remembers it.]*

We were fishing up at Bristol Bay west of Port Moeller about 70 miles. We had just finished filling the boat with 130,000 pounds of crab. It had been a long, 10-day grind to put that crab on there.

The whole 10 days it was blowing northwest at 40 up to about 70, back to 40—it was awful weather.

Anyway we finished up our trip and were heading for Unimak Pass and ultimately for King Cove to unload. I was on the wheel; the crew was buttoning up the deck getting ready to go in. I plotted a course, looking pretty carefully at what the tide was going to be doing. I wanted to get to Unimak Pass right at slack high water. You don't want to be in the pass on the flood tide with a northwest wind going. Then it's the wind against the current, and the seas get flat ugly in those conditions.

We had the weather quartering our starboard stern *[the wind and waves were coming at the boat diagonally from the right rear]*. The course was doable and safe—I ran it for about an hour checking it out to make sure. I was running 1,350 *[engine revolutions per minute]*, making 7 knots *[nautical miles per hour—about 8 "land" miles per hour]*. It wasn't too fast for conditions but was enough power to keep steerage and maintain course. I felt safe. The seas were probably 20 to 25 feet, and it was blowing northwest 40 to 45. It was not nice, but we're pretty seaworthy—I've got water in the tanks, so we've got a lot of weight below the waterline.

I was dead tired—I'd been up a couple days. So after I saw we were riding just fine I called Scotty Templin and my daughter, Nicole, to take wheel watch and I went to bed. I was going to lie down for a couple hours before we got to the pass, and then I'd take watch when we went through the pass.

I wasn't down very long when that wave hit us. If you look at the video, it looks like we're right in the trough *[with the waves coming directly at the side of the boat, making it vulnerable to a rollover]*. After I laid down I think the wind changed direction a little bit. I think it started coming more out of the west. I would never have deliberately put us on a course in the gash or in the trough like that.

That wave hit us so hard that it rolled the boat over on the port side so far that the engines all died due to loss of oil pressure. When they're tipped on their side like that, the oil all runs out of the oil pan, the oil pump loses suction, and that triggers an automatic shutoff so you don't burn the engines up.

"All you could hear was the wind screaming."
The wave threw me out of my bunk, over the walkway between it and the desk, and onto the desk on the port wall of my stateroom. That's where I woke up. The generators had just quit, so it was pitch-black. I was completely disoriented because the wall was the floor, and for a minute I couldn't tell which way was up. The engines were dead, and all you could hear was the wind screaming.

I thought we'd hit either another boat or that we'd hit a rock and were on the beach—I wasn't sure which. When I finally made it to the wheelhouse I was sure I was going to see the rigging of another boat tangled up in ours, but there was nothing there.

I said, "What the hell happened?"

Scotty said, "We took a *huge* wave, man."

We took out a window—that's the worst on a boat. I'm wet, the floor's wet, there's water everywhere, there's no window. I'm yelling at the engineer to get engines started, 'cause without the circ pumps going, we've got slack tanks. When the tanks go down, water can shift to one side, and that'll roll you over. They call it having too much free surface. It's a death sentence. You have to have tanks pressed full of water. If they're half full, you're done.

[Down in the engine room, the engineer has to make a quick decision: Which of the many stalled engines should he get going first? The generators so the circ pumps can fill up the tanks and prevent a potential rollover and so the skipper and crew can see what was going on? Or the main engines so the boat can regain forward momentum? It's a close call because even with the mains going, the boat's servo-operated rudders won't function until the generators get back on line. The engineer's gut reaction is to start the two big mains first—a decision Corky is grateful for back up in the pilothouse.]

The only thing worse than freezing sea spray: frozen sea spray. A coating of sea ice makes deck work even more treacherous—and can sink a boat if too thick.

The engineer got the mains going first. I'm so disoriented, I hardly know what I'm doing. We've got no instrumentation, I've got no steering because I've got no generator, so I'm trying to twin-screw us into the sea.

[Although he can't even see which way the seas are coming from in the inky dark, as soon as the engines rumble to life, Corky uses a technique normally reserved for docking a twin-engined boat or for sidling up to a pot: maneuvering with the engines alone. He puts one engine full ahead and slams the other full astern, trying to spin the boat with pure engine torque and propeller thrust so the bow faces into the seas. It works.]

We finally got the generator started up. I got my steering back and started jogging into it to get my wits about me.

[Only then, with the power on, the boat under relative control, and the pilothouse lights back on, does Corky get a look at how bad the damage is.]

Under the dash is an 8D heavy-duty emergency battery. It's a lead-acid battery just like a car battery except it weighs over 100 pounds. The wave had flipped it out of its holder, and it was upside down under the dash. Battery acid was running out all over the floor—you could smell it. We opened the door, grabbed it, and flipped it back upright. We had no computer—both of our computers were out, and one was all wet.

Then I took a look at the window. It's made of bulletproof, 3/8-inch Lexan. The wave hit the window so hard, it didn't shatter or break—it actually stretched it in and ripped around all four corners like paper. It just caved in like a bubble. Enough water came through those four small rips to completely soak the wheelhouse. I shoved paper towels into the four corners where the cracks were.

"As near as I can figure."

At this point you hear me say on the tape that I didn't think we'd have any current problems, but that evidently I was wrong. I'm still half asleep at that point and figuring we took a wave because we're too close to the pass while the current was running. But I soon figured out we were still a long way from the pass. As near as I can figure, it was a damn rogue wave. If you look at the video of that thing coming at us, it had to be 60 feet tall.

I didn't go back to sleep for the next 14 hours until we were in the flat calm of Unimak bight. The seas were big, and it wasn't real comfortable, but it was doable. Typical Bering Sea, nothing out of the norm.

Working at the rail, fishermen have to keep one eye on their work and another on the horizon. A rogue wave can materialize almost any time.

"The biggest rescue of them all."
—Captain Phil Harris

My dad was in the biggest rescue of them all, on the *Golden Viking*. He blew all the windows out. It shot glass through two different walls, across the stateroom—it was unbelievable. He was missing for eight days, and the Coast Guard was looking for him. Everybody was looking, and nobody could find him. I was in Seattle, so on the eighth day I got one of the families together and said, "Look, we're going to have to start making funeral arrangements because they're gone." It was my dad and a couple of my best friends.

And about six in the morning on a Sunday, it was just turning light and one of the guys on the processor ship was in shaving. I'll never forget it—he said he looked out the window and he cut himself; he couldn't believe what he'd seen. It was my dad on *Golden Viking*. All the windows are blown out, the whole bow's caved in. A big wave had come and just engulfed the boat. He did a million dollars' worth of damage to it but he saved everybody's life.

When the wave hit, it took out all the controls. When that happens all the engines go to full throttle—they run away, we call it. You have to manually shut them down immediately or they'll blow up. Meanwhile all the generators are shorted out but still pumping out power so everything's live—you can't touch any metal on the boat, or you'll get shocked if not fried.

So he had to get all that stabilized, then jury-rig some hand throttles and get it in gear, and rig up the hand-steering, and start jogging toward town. He could only make one or two miles an hour so it took him eight days. But he was smart enough and good enough to make it. He was looking at the stars and looking at the moon to navigate—he had nothing: no radio, no electronics, no compass. He had a steering wheel, and that was it.

He got all cut up. When the glass came flying by him, it mostly missed him but it just sliced the hell out of his ears.

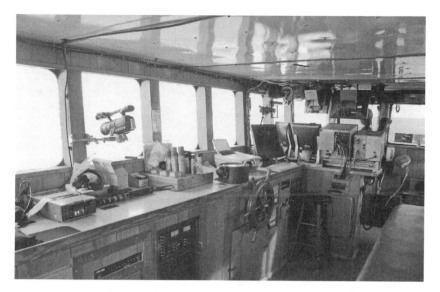

Captain Phil Harris has seen it all from the wheelhouse of *Cornelia Marie*. TV fans get the same view, thanks to cameras mounted alongside the windows.

"I'm going to die!"
—*Captain Phil Harris*

A boat had a wave take a window out, and the boat was on its side and sinking. The VHF *[marine radio]* was stuck on channel 16 so you could hear all the screaming and yelling going on as guys tried to get out alive.

The only way out of that boat was through the wheelhouse window. The boat is on its side, and the guys are going out the window. The last guy was the engineer, and he was too big to get out the window.

You can hear him in the wheelhouse screaming and yelling that he was going to die: "I've got a family! I've got kids! I'm going to die!"

He's alone in a sinking boat with water pouring in, talking to himself, realizing that he's about to die.

The whole fleet's hearing his last words because that radio was stuck on, and there was nothing anybody could do about it. And he died because he couldn't fit through the window.

SINKINGS

Waves are only one way to sink a boat. As the following two stories show, something as dramatic as hitting an uncharted reef or as subtle as an undetectable leak can also drag a crabber to the bottom. Both incidents pitted the professionalism, ingenuity, guts, and stamina of the crew against a deadly enemy in an ultimate-stakes game of survival.

"We all would have drowned"
—Captain Corky Tilley

We were fishing tanner crab on the west side of Kodiak in February 1985. We did really good. Had a hell of a season. The owner of the boat gave me *El Rancho*, an 86-foot crabber, and we fished about a week. We had 30,000 pounds of tanner crab on when it started to blow. It was blowing 70 or 80 southwest, so we went in to anchor and wait for the blow to go by. I got up next morning and started heading across Lower Shelikov toward Kodiak. We had all the gear on the boat, so we were heavy. We had just finished dinner, and everyone was sleeping but the engineer and me. I was sitting on wheel watch, had my stocking feet up on the dash when I noticed the boat was starting to list.

With a full load of gear you tend to roll, and we were starting to roll a bit heavy to starboard. There was about a 15- or 20-foot swell. I told the engineer to transfer some fuel to the port side. *[Crab boats typically have several fuel tanks. To help balance the boat, the engineer can operate pumps to transfer fuel from tanks on one side of the boat to tanks on the other.]*

He said, "I *have* been transferring to port."

Well, I woke up the whole crew right away. As they're coming up to the wheelhouse, I told the engineer to go back down and check his valves and make sure the fuel was going where he thought it was and to come right back up and let me know.

[The engineer double- and triple-checks the valves, and there is no mistake: He's been pumping thousands of gallons of fuel out of

the starboard tank and into the port tank. According to logic the boat should be listing to port but it is still leaning the other way.]

"I've got a starboard list and I can't figure out why."
A buddy of mine was fishing pollack in Shelikof Straits. I'd been talking to him on the radio so I told him what was going on: "I've got a starboard list and I can't figure out why."

Either the gear has shifted or we're taking on water—and the gear was fine. Without calling the Coast Guard I gave my buddy my position, then went about trying to figure out what was wrong.

[Corky then goes about a calm, systematic, almost scientific search for why his boat is acting like a doomed ship. He had all his pots on deck, but they were well stacked and lashed down tight, so Corky rules out a gear problem. That means there had to be a leak somewhere. The engine room is the lowest point in the ship and the place the water would turn up first from just about any leak. But it is fine. None of the bilge alarms—devices that sense water in the bottom of the hull—are going off either. Yet the boat continues to lean harder and harder to starboard as though it is preparing for a death roll.

Corky is already a veteran fisherman with 20 years at sea under his belt. He's been on plenty of leaky boats and endured lots of close calls before and he's not one to start hollering "Mayday!" when something gets a little bit out of the ordinary. On the other hand he's seen and heard lots of boats go down and lost more than a few friends to the Bering Sea. His quick, calm response to the situation is a textbook look at a professional at work.]

By now we're listing pretty bad, so I slowed the boat down, turned into the waves, and told the crew to get their survival suits out. I had no idea we were going to be abandoning ship; I'm just taking precautionary measures.

[Boats typically start listing slowly. But if the cause of the list can't be found and corrected relatively early on, the listing

129

accelerates as the boat becomes increasingly unbalanced. Once
Corky has exhausted all means to find the problem, he knows their
time afloat could be limited.]

It was starting to freak me out—the bilge was dry, no alarms were
going off, but I was obviously taking on water somewhere on the
starboard side, and it's only getting worse. We're listing further and
further to starboard.

[Corky continues to rack his brain and sift the evidence for any
possible explanation for the boat's list. At the same time he continues
preparing to abandon ship.]

I had this great big giant on the crew. His nickname was Crane.
He was strong as a bull. I tell him, "Crane, jump up on the roof and
grab the life raft." It was a huge raft; no ordinary man could have
picked that thing up and gotten it off the roof.

[Life rafts on modern crab boats are inflatable survival vessels

tightly packed into large, lozenge-shape fiberglass capsules.
They're strapped to the highest point on the boat: the pilothouse
roof. Ingeniously designed, they automatically break free of their
mountings and float to the surface if the boat sinks. The raft capsule,
however, remains tethered to the sinking boat by a 60-foot lanyard.
When the boat passes the 60-foot mark on its way to the bottom, the
lanyard pulls tight, activating a cartridge of compressed gas inside
the capsule. The cartridge blows the capsule apart, simultaneously
inflating the raft.

The 60-foot "fuse" between the sinking boat and the inflating
raft is designed to prevent the raft from inflating too soon and
getting tangled or damaged in the boat's rigging. There's a
downside to this delay, however: If a boat is going down slowly,
it can leave the crew in the water without a raft for some time. In
heavy seas such as those El Rancho *finds herself in, that delay*
can be enough to scatter the crew—and staying together is their
best chance of survival. When the raft eventually inflates, it may
be too far away to be useful.

If he were going to abandon ship, Corky wants to to inflate the
lifeboat manually with a tug on the lanyard as soon as El Rancho's
rigging disappears beneath the surface so he can get all his men in
the raft immediately.]

Crane was on the port side with the life raft; all the crew had
survival suits on. We're now listing so far over, I can hear stuff
falling off shelves and out of lockers. I've got to make the call as to
when to get off this boat. So I tell the crew I'm hearing stuff crashing
and that we'd better get out. It was time to call the Coast Guard.

"Mayday! Mayday! Mayday! We're going to go over!"
[The survival-suited crew leaves the pilothouse to join Crane on the
port rail—now the highest point of the boat. Corky is the only man
on board who's not in a survival suit, as he's been too busy to put
one on. He remains in the pilothouse just long enough to make El
Rancho's *last radio transmission.]*

"Mayday! Mayday! Mayday! *El Rancho*! We're going to go over!
The boat has a bad starboard list! We're going to go over!" And I
gave my position. Then the boat took a big heave over to starboard,
and I was *not* going to be trapped in that wheelhouse, so I got the
hell out of there. I knew that my buddy had my position so I wasn't
worried about it.

[Then Corky scrambles for his life, out of the wheelhouse and
onto the steeply slanting deck.]

The Coast Guard called back right away. *"El Rancho! El*
Rancho!"—I could hear them on the pilothouse radio but I couldn't
answer—I'm outside and I had to get my survival suit on. We were
going to roll over any moment.

[Fishermen routinely drill donning survival suits when in port.
On a level dock in calm weather, the fishermen unroll the thick,
bulky suits, climb into them like overalls, zip up the closures, don the
insulated hoods, and fasten the watertight seal around the mouth and
neck, leaving only the nose and eyes exposed. Anything under one

minute is considered a good time. Corky climbs into his and seals it in less than 15 seconds.

Then he makes the hardest decision of his career.]

That was the scariest part—making the decision to jump off a boat that's still floating. I don't want to have someone radio in: "Hey, I seen your boat floating." You look like an idiot. On the other hand you can get caught in the rigging and get dragged down with the boat if you jump too late. It was the most agonizing call. But the list was getting so bad so fast, I knew it was just a matter of time before we went over.

"Jump in! Get in the water!"

I told the crew: "OK, we're all going to get out at once. Crane, throw the raft in the water"— So Crane throws the raft in—"and follow me." And then I jump into the ocean. I jump; Crane and the engineer jump in with me. The other two are walking down the side of the boat but they're not getting in. It's February, it's probably 25 degrees. It's gonna be cold in there. So I tell 'em: "Jump in! Get in the water!" And they finally did. Right after we cleared the boat, it rolled over.

When the boat rolled over and sank, I was halfway relieved, because then I knew I'd made the right call. I knew if I hadn't woken up the crew when I first noticed the problem, if I hadn't gotten everyone in a suit and gotten the life raft down, we all would have drowned.

[The life raft, however, is still just a bobbing fiberglass capsule. Corky knows he has to inflate it fast so the crew can get in while they're still close by.]

I got the lanyard from the raft and I am pulling it, but nothing's happening. It's pitch-black out—I can't see my hand in front of my face, it's so dark. The lanyard is around my head, over my arms—I'm all tangled up in it. The survival suit is over my mouth, so I can't breathe real well, and I'm breathing real hard anyway— my boat just sank, and I'm trying to get this raft to pop. And who comes and grabs hold of me? Crane. He's freakin' out! He tries to climb up on me to get out of the water. Well, he's pushing me under so I can't breathe. I say, "Crane! Get the hell away from me! Hang onto the raft! I've got to get the raft up!"

[The survival suits are flotation devices as well as protection from the frigid water, but the natural instinct to climb to high ground is a strong one. Crane obediently lets go of his skipper but latches onto the life raft canister with a powerful bear hug. Meanwhile Corky is still struggling to pop the raft open, but each yank on the cord just jerks the hermetically sealed canister toward him.]

I finally realize I got to get on my back, put my feet against the raft, take a wrap of the cord around my hand, and pull as hard as I can.

BOOM! The raft goes off, and Crane ends up inside it. I don't know if it inflated under him or what. I climb in with him. There's a little tiny light on top, and we look around for the others.

"I can't make it!"

[Corky's decision to have Crane get the raft—and his own struggle with the inflation lanyard—pays off. Before El Rancho's *lights dim beneath them, the raft is open, its light is on, and in its glow Corky can see that the crew is all nearby. The deckhand farthest away is only 30 or 40 feet from the raft, but he seems paralyzed with fear.]*

I called out to him to move his arms. But he was freaking out. "I can't make it!" he was saying, "I can't make it!" I told him to move his arms and swim this way, but he just kept saying, "I can't! I can't!"

"Swim over to that guy and tow him over here!" I told the engineer, and he did, and we got him in. That deckhand was a big, strong kid and in good shape. But he was going into shock and he thought we were all going to die.

I was telling him: "I see lights, boats are coming. The Coast Guard is going to come get us. It's going to be OK." But he was visibly shaken. He doesn't fish anymore; he works in a cannery, I think.

[Without Corky's decades of experience at sea, the panicked deckhand's reaction is quite understandable: He knows that many crabbers who lose their boats lose their lives shortly thereafter. Awakened from sleep to find the boat listing, the skipper baffled, and no help in sight, it's no wonder that he concludes certain death is at hand.]

The raft was not the most comfortable thing. These rollers were crashing through the door and over the top of the raft. The raft is full of water, and we could feel our legs start to get cold through our survival suits. But we were in an enclosure and together.

[Those two facts are a huge advantage: Life rafts are large and easy for rescuers to spot. They're covered with a canopy to reduce weather exposure. Finding an entire crew in one location means they're far more likely to all get picked up quickly in one trip and are less likely to perish of hypothermia or drift off while rescuers are attending to other crew scattered about the ocean. And crew members together in a life raft can keep morale up and tend to any crewmen who go into shock.]

Once we were in the raft, I was totally content and happy with my situation. I knew I'd made the right decision to abandon ship. I knew I was going to live. I knew I was no longer on a boat that was going to roll over. I had no worry about my position being found: We're on the 100-fathom edge southwest of Alitak Bay. I think that would put us 25 or 30 miles off the beach, in lower Shelikof. I'm sitting in the doorway of the raft and after about an hour I could see the C-130 *[Coast Guard rescue plane]* circling. I shot off a few flares to make sure they see us. I can see the lights of boats coming. I know we're going to be fine.

But the deckhand was still in shock. I kept telling him we were going to be OK. That didn't seem to help much, so then I started telling jokes for him, trying to keep him humored. The engineer and a couple of them were laughing, but the deckhand isn't taking it too well. He wanted out of that raft.

[Soon enough the crew gets their wish: A Coast Guard

helicopter arrives, hovers overhead, and lowers a rescue basket to
the men in the raft.]

Nowadays they send a rescue swimmer down to hook you up, to
get you in the basket, but they didn't back then. The basket is coming
down at you and swinging around on the cable in big 12-foot arcs.
Swooosh! like that. And we're surfing down the waves in this raft. I
was at the door of the raft, catching the basket. One by one the guys
get in the basket, and I motion the helo for them to take 'em up. First
one out of the raft is the deckhand.

[With his crew safely in the chopper, it's now Corky's turn. With
no one to hold the basket for him, he has to try to stabilize it and at
the same time climb in—all this in heavy seas that jerk the basket
out of his hands and send it catapulting over the waves. Finally
Corky manages to get most of his body in the basket, and the helo
starts reeling him in.

These baskets are pretty small and light. They're aluminum. And
I'm in this Gumby suit and mostly underwater so I'm having trouble
feeling with my body whether I'm in the basket or not. Well I wasn't
quite all the way in. When they pull you up they pull you up hard.
The basket is still swinging—it's terrifying. It took me up 15 feet—
and I fell out of the basket and landed on my back in the ocean again.
It knocked the wind out of me.

I can't breathe, I'm trying to get back to the raft. And right about when
I get to the raft, here comes this damn basket—*Feeeeoow!*—right by my
head. They're lowering the basket again but they nearly killed me the first
time, so I want no part of it. I wave the helo off. I can see the glow of lights
on the horizon. I know boats are coming. I'm thinking, "No! Go!"

But they wouldn't leave. They come back again, they drop the
basket on me, and it's either grab the basket or get hit in the head with
it, so I grab it and I realize I've got no choice but to get in it or they'll
keep dropping it on me. So I got in it or mostly. How I don't know.

Then BAM! I'm 100 feet up in the air just like that, looking at the
little white light of the raft way down there. It's scary as hell! They

pulled me up so fast, they cracked a couple of my ribs because I wasn't in quite right.

On the flight back the commander chewed me out for waving off the helo. He said, "My crew risked their lives to get you guys, that's just plain disrespectful." I tried to explain that if he were in my shoes he'd have done the same thing. I'd much rather have gotten on a crab boat than on that basket.

[Corky gets off the chopper in Kodiak in bare feet. Before he can even get a coat and some shoes to wear, the Coast Guard interrogates him about what happened. It's something they're obliged to do to make sure there is no insurance fraud.]

They cross-examined me from every angle. Let's put it this way: If I had sunk that boat on purpose, they would have known it. But there's only one way it went down, and that's the way it went down.

[How El Rancho *went down is pretty straightforward. But why it went down continues to mystify and torment Corky long after he is safely ashore. It almost becomes a preoccupation.]*

I finally figured out that there were voids that run the length of the boat on each side of the hull. These voids didn't have pumps; they had drains that were supposed to drain the water into the engine room bilge, where the bilge pumps would pump it overboard. Somehow that starboard void had a leak in it. Maybe it filled through a hatch, maybe the hull had a crack in it somewhere. Anyway for some reason it was filling up, and the more we listed, the more it took on water.

The hole that was supposed to drain it was just a nipple of 1-inch pipe, and there were planks down the length of that void you could walk down to inspect it. Well maybe a chunk of cardboard or wood or even a paper bag plugged it, and water came in and couldn't drain out. Our crab tanks were already full of crab and water; we were fully loaded with gear. Hell if you'd spilled coffee in the engine room you might have sank. You were already three-quarters sunk.

"We put four holes in the bottom."
—Lenny Lekanoff

We got close to an island, bumped an uncharted reef, and put four holes in the bottom of the boat. As soon as we felt it and the bilge alarms went off, we knew what had happened, so we headed out into open water again so we wouldn't do any more damage to the hull. The skipper put it on autopilot, real slow, and we all headed down to the engine room to check it out.

[Putting holes in the middle of the boat can be a death sentence. Crab boats are big compared to pleasure boats but tiny by commercial vessel standards. They typically have very few watertight compartments—generally only two at the most: one in the very front of the boat and one in the very back. Getting holed anywhere in the middle of the hull generally means that unless you can somehow stop the flow of water, you're going down. The more holes, the greater the danger, as you have to divide manpower between several damaged areas.

Modern crab boats are steel, which makes emergency repairs to a hull difficult if not impossible. Rips and bends in plate steel require a dry dock to fix.]

We found two leaks in the forward portion of the boat right away. They were pretty bad. By the time we got pumps going in there, the engine room bilge alarms are going off. So we run in there and start pulling up floorboards to see what the problem is there and we see two more places where water is coming in real good.

["Real good" is an understatement. Hitting the reef has dented the plate steel hull, breaking the welds where the hull fastens to the boat's ribs. The result is two foot-long cracks ranging from an inch to a few inches wide at the very bottom of the boat—right where the water pressure is greatest and the tears are most difficult to access. Now water roars in a sheet that threatens to fill the boat in minutes.

To survive, the crew has to do two things: get the water out of the boat as fast as it comes in and plug the holes. First order is to start pumping. Normally the boat sucks in seawater to fill the crab tanks and cool the various engines. In an emergency the crab tanks can be sealed and the pumps' suction diverted to the bilge.]

It was coming in so fast that we had every pump sucking water out of the bilge and over the side—the crab tank pumps, the heat-exchanger pumps on the main engine.... We even ran all the generators and had their water pumps, their engine cooling pumps, pushing water over the side. We even ran the *spare* auxiliary engine just to have water going through its heat exchanger. We were scrambling.

[Even with every pump on the boat running hard, they can't keep up with the leaks. The water in the engine room is knee-deep and getting deeper. It's a matter of life or death to slow down the leaks before the water gets deep enough to stall the engines. No engines, no pumps. No pumps, and down you go. Fast.

Most boats have a damage control kit. In contrast to all the high-tech safety mechanisms—the automatic bilge pumps, the electronic bilge alarms, the remote cameras that keep an eye out for incoming water—the damage control kit is relatively Stone Age: On many boats it consists of a bucket of wooden plugs and wedges of various sizes and shapes, designed to be pounded into any tears or holes in the hull in a desperate, last-ditch effort to save the vessel. It is exactly what Lenny's boat needs most. And they don't have one.]

We started tearing deck boards, anything and everything made of wood that we could find, cutting it into foot-long pieces, splitting it, cutting it into wedges so we could drive them into the holes.

[Of course all the time spent ripping and sawing and splitting only allows more water to come in. By the time the crew has wood to work with, they are already soaked, their arms and legs numb from feeling around in the sloshing bilge to find the cracks and estimate by the incoming torrent how large and wide they are. The water is now 4 feet deep and rising.]

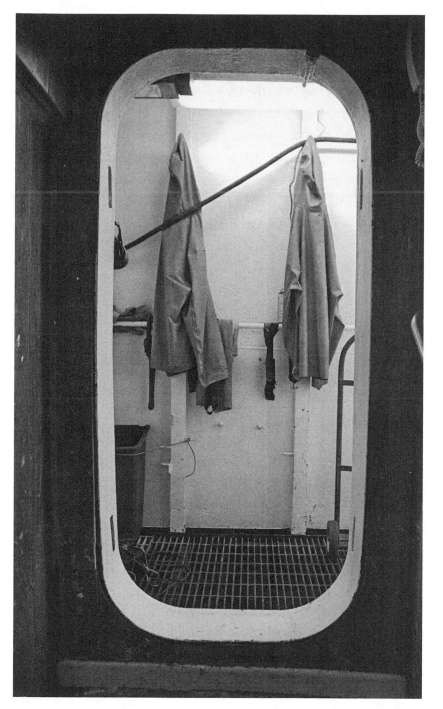

Watertight companionways give crewmembers access to sections of the ship that can be sealed off from flooding.

Then we crawled down into the bilge and kept jamming pieces of wood in the holes. We'd wedge them in, then pound them in as far as we could with 5-pound sledgehammers. The pumps were just keeping the water down to the level where you could just barely reach in and hammer. Your arm would get numb from the cold and the hammering, until you couldn't hold the hammer anymore. You'd give it to someone else and go on deck and try to help someone else rip up some more deck boards. It took us a whole day to do that, rotating guys in and out of the bilge every few minutes before we had it shored up enough so that the coolant pumps could keep up with the leak and we could finally head into town. That was a day and a half away. Another boat followed us in.

It was quite a scare. There's a certain point you get to when you know you can beat it, and that's what everybody was working to do. We probably didn't sleep for 36 hours. Even after we had plugged it as well as we could, we had two guys always in the engine room to make sure the plugs were staying in, to hammer them back in if they started working loose.

You would never think this little emergency kit could save a boat until you experience it like I did. But it can. They're required nowadays. We have one on *Wizard*, lots of plugs, and wedges, and stuff. I'm glad to have that around.

MAN OVERBOARD!

Immersion in icy water can kill nearly immediately—faster in many cases than a deadly poison or a gunshot. As soon as a body hits the water, it goes into a disabling mental and physical shock. Within seconds, it becomes difficult to move, then virtually impossible. In a very few minutes, hypothermia is fatal. It's quite probable that you're better off being bitten by a rattlesnake in the wilderness than being dropped fully-clothed into the Bering Sea. Some men barely survive a dunking, thanks to the help of their quick-acting fellow crewmen; many are less fortunate.

"Heeeellllppp!"
—Monte Colburn

My first day fishing the boat was anchored out on the harbor alongside the boat my brother was working on. The two boats were tied together.

We were all crossing back and forth from one boat to another, just kind of goofing off, hanging out, taking the day off. So I went to go jump across and somehow I ended up in the water between the two boats. The skipper said it was an absolute miracle that I didn't get killed, because when you tie boats up like that anchored out, they're constantly surging and smashing against each other. And this was the middle of winter while we were waiting out a storm.

Well I was dressed appropriately for the middle of February in the Bering Sea. I had Sorel boots on, a Powderhorn jacket, a camera. *[He laughs.]* I was loaded down pretty well.

[Monte's brother, Keith, interrupts him: "He was dressed with everything that you would want if you were going to go tromping around through the snow somewhere. It's not what you wear on a crab boat."]

There are big rubber buoys between the boats that try to keep the boats from going steel to steel and hitting each other. I was in the water lunging up, trying to grab a hold of one of these buoys.

Crab-pot buoys serve as fenders when boats are tied to one another. Grabbing one on the way down may be a falling crewman's last chance at survival.

After three or four attempts it became pretty clear to me that I didn't have a whole lot of chances left. You hit 30-degree water, your body goes into shock right away. You start to stiffen up. You get hypothermic. I was starting to get really concerned that I wasn't going to be able to get a hold of the buoy.

Finally I *did* manage to get a hold of the buoy, and I climbed up, and I was sitting on it. Soaking wet of course. As I was sitting there, the thought ran through my mind that, well, maybe I can just climb up and sneak up on board and nobody will know. I was embarrassed to say the least. And that thought lasted about a half a second, and my next thought was to scream, "Heeeelllllppp!"

A couple of guys came out and they looked over the side and they looked down at me and they said, "What the hell are you doing down there?"

I was damn lucky.

"Then his hand came up out of the water . . ."
—Captain Keith Colburn

We were tied in Dutch Harbor, and another boat was lying outside of us. We had a big stack of gear on the boat, as did they, and I was sitting in the wheelhouse. Everyone else was down in the galley, and I watched these two kids come climbing across. It was about 8 or 9 at night, and one kid jumped up on our stack, and he grabbed the sling that's in the crane hook. But he grabbed the wrong end of it so he pulled it right out of the hook. He hit the stack, trampolined down over the side and between the boats. Both boats have a 6- or 7-foot shelter wall, so there's like a narrow steel canyon there ending in the water. His head bounced off both sides. It sounded like someone threw a bowling ball down between the boats.

His buddy jumped down there, and I went down the house and grabbed a couple guys and ran outside. The kid was gone; we couldn't see him. His buddy had jumped down on a buoy to try to help him, but there was nobody there to help. Then his hand came up out of the water just like this eerie, slow, last-gasp type of deal, and we all grabbed him and pulled him aboard. He'd hit his head on the way down, and his eyes were all glassy and cross-eyed. It was all he could do to raise that one hand, and that saved him. Luckily he came out of it OK but he was awfully close to becoming a statistic.

The second year that I was on the boat was the year *Top Gun* was playing, so guys were calling each other Ice, Goose, and Maverick. Rocket, Billy, and another guy they called Ice were coming back from the bar one night in the middle of February and crossing the boats. The last thing Billy said to Ice before he jumped from one boat to another was one of the lines out of the movie: "Just a walk in the park, guys." Well Billy made it across, but Ice slipped, fell, went down between the boats, and they never saw him. They tried to get to him but they never found him. Divers dragged him out of the harbor dead the next morning.

"I'd give everything . . . to get that one life back."

—Captain Larry Hendricks

We were jogging into a storm. The weather was so bad, we needed three of us in the wheelhouse just to watch for waves. We hear a "Mayday!" from a friend's boat saying they lost two and maybe three guys overboard. We set our course to head that way, but after two minutes going that direction, we know we're not going to survive if we keep heading that way—we'll be in the same fix as the other boat.

We knew our friend was dying, and we had to turn back.

[Larry can barely choke out his next few sentences.]

You hear that on the radio, and you can't help, and you get tears in your eyes, and you don't know how to handle it.

His name was Scottie Powell. I have a picture of him on my bulletin board. I never will forget him. On the radio I'm waiting to hear the name of the guy on the boat that's lost. I know 'em all. I don't want it to be any of 'em, but Scottie, I'd fished with most, I was closest to. You hear the name, your heart sinks. There's nothing you can do. You're so helpless. You wish it never happened.

I'd give up everything good that ever happened to me to get that one life back.

It's the nature of our work. We could be a memory at some time ourselves. To keep a sane mind you have to be like a fireman or a cop. You can't think about it. It affects everybody different. I've been running a boat twice with guys on board who have had brothers on other boats that went down. I find out on the radio, and those guys are out on deck working. How do I tell them? What do I do? It's mind-boggling.

Our family lost 14 men in the '80s. We took a month off to try to recuperate. At the end of the month, we're steaming back up to the fishing grounds, and a life raft pops up next to us. It's a raft from one of the boats, and it took us all back to square one again. Why? Nobody knows.

Where it all begins: Dutch Harbor, Alaska, is the *Deadliest Catch* fleet's jumping-off point in the Bering Sea.

Maverick plies flat-calm water—an unusual condition in the Bering Sea.

Cornelia Marie is laden with crab pots as she heads out to sea.

Northwestern's high bow was designed to ride big waves.

Time Bandit was fisherman-designed for extreme stability in rough weather.

Sorting crab on deck aboard *Time Bandit* goes pretty smoothly in calm seas. When the weather gets rough, it's another story.

Moving pots on deck while taking heavy spray is like trying to work while being blasted with a fire hose. For Bering Sea deckhands, it's just another day on the job.

Deckhand Matt Bradley throws a crab-pot buoy seaward.

Launching a pot takes brawn, guts, skill, timing, and coordination.

Two crewmen hold onto a pot as a wave threatens to knock them off their feet.

Been there, filmed that: a *Deadliest Catch* photographer at work.

Time Bandit's crew struggles to pull a pot before being slammed by the next big wave, already looming high over the bow.

Northwestern pulls a pot jammed with crab.

As the hull of their boat heaves and gyrates beneath their feet, a crab-boat crew lands their catch.

A full pot of crab hitting the sorting table is music to the ears of a crab fisherman.

Smaller but more numerous than their larger cousins, opilio crabs offer a second chance for crab-boat crews to strike it rich on the Bering Sea.

Josh and Jake Harris grab a piece of what it's all about: a lunker red crab.

Sorting hundreds of opilio crab per pot is a welcome chore: Fishing is good.

Deckhand Brian Greer prepares to set a pot from the pitching aft deck of *Rollo*.

Crabbers often work round-the-clock, on decks lit to near daylight levels by big sodium floodlights. Here, *Northwestern*'s crew prepares to launch a crab pot.

Suspended over a frigid and frothing sea, *Deadliest Catch* photographer Todd Stanley goes for the high angle while shooting deck action from a crab boat crane.

As a crab pot and buoy head overboard, a crane-riding cameraman is there to capture the action for television viewers.

Two *Deadliest Catch* crew members prepare to launch the show's submarine, which accounts for some of the most amazing television images.

"This is a story that really bothers me."
—*Captain Phil Harris*

This is a story that really bothers me. We hired a guy by the name of Mike, probably in '82 or '83. He was my age. His wife was over at her mom's house, and they had a newborn. She called Mike and said, "I'll bring a pizza home for dinner." On the way home she was hit by a drunk driver and she and their baby were killed.

Mike kind of went berserk and he wound up on skid row. One of my dad's partners found him and saw that he was a pretty good guy, cleaned him up, and he turns out to be a great deckhand. He and I worked together on deck for about three years when he met a girl and they were going to get married. He and I were real good friends and he asked me to be his best man. Everybody was pulling for him because they knew what had happened to him.

Right before he was going to get married, we flew him up to do this quick blue crab trip. Blue crab season only lasts four or five days, so he was just going to run up, do this trip, and come home and get married. Well the boat rolled over, and two guys made it out, but everybody else drowned—and Mike was one of the guys who drowned. It happened right in front of me. I'm looking at the boat upside down, just the hull, and I know those guys are alive under there, but there's nothing anybody can do.

It kind of got to me, you know?

Then the very next year we lost a guy off the *Golden Viking* and we never found him. This stuff happens to you, and if you take it personally, it will drive you insane.

I don't really get emotional about a lot of things that most people do, because if I let it get to me I probably couldn't do this job. You start to get numb to losing guys. You have to. A bunch of my friends have drowned doing this, but Mike was probably the one that bothered me the most.

"Every decision you make is a life-or-death deal."

—Captain Phil Harris

You always tell these guys, "Never go outside by yourself." But after we'd left Seattle, one guy went outside by himself—nobody knew he was out there. He climbed up on a stack of pots, and he was going to paint and clean in the back of the boat. He fell off and we didn't know it for five or 10 minutes. I am always taking a head count, always paying attention to who's doing what, and I didn't see him, and so—I don't know why—I stopped the boat right away. I said, "Let's quick look everywhere we can," and within minutes we knew he was gone. I called the Coast Guard right then, and sure as hell he was gone.

That's a brutal feeling to live with. Because you think it's your fault. I didn't do anything wrong, but you can't convince yourself of that at the time. All you know is that they're dead, they're gone. Then you pray that somehow he made it to the beach, because we were only a half mile from the beach—but no, we never found him.

He was the second of two sons that were killed inside a month of each other, and his mom lost it and charged me with murder. She said that we went out and killed him. The Coast Guard investigated the whole thing and said we'd done everything right. It was an accident. But his mom was just so whacked out, she'd write the Coast Guard letters that said her son was going to come back and walk across the water, and he's going to tell everybody what really happened.

And the Coast Guard said, "Well, we know what really happened. And the crew and captain didn't have anything to do with anything. It was an accident."

I was cleared of everything. The investigators came in and they said: "You were exemplary, you did a perfect job." And then it was dropped. But it still . . . in your mind you wonder whether you did something wrong. Every day every decision you make is a life-and-death deal.

FREAK OCCURRENCES

The dangers of crabbing are almost too numerous to relate. Here are a few that almost defy classification.

Although perishing from fire when surrounded by ice water seems so contradictory as to be impossible, it is a frequent killer at sea. Other elements that are relatively benign ashore, such as engine breakdowns and toothaches, become big deals at sea. Other incidents related here are simply bizarre: Who'd think you could get nearly sucked to death for instance—or experience an event that bordered on the paranormal while trying to find shelter in a storm?

"Just like the movie *Inferno*."
—Captain Larry Hendricks

Fire is a real danger. I had this greenhorn cook one time, and he started a fire. He shut off all the lights, the stove, everything. Well, in a boat at sea you need to keep the generators running to keep exhaust flowing out the pipe, or you can take a wave, and water can fill up the stacks and fill up the engine. And you need to keep a load on the generator or you've got too much free power, and that can burn up wiring too.

Well, the greenhorn turned everything off, and then when he came back in, he turned the stove on high. It had never been run on high— since it was always on, you didn't need to. There was 30 years of grease accumulated behind that stove. I went in and smelled smoke and opened the oven door, and suddenly it was just like the movie *Inferno*. Solid flame. The engine room blower filled the pilothouse with so much smoke, I couldn't even find the radio mikes so I could broadcast a mayday.

We were way up in the ice, and the Coast Guard said, "We can't get to you—we're 300 miles away." So I radioed the nearest boat and said, "I can't even see the inside of the wheelhouse. We have to evacuate. Look for us on an ice floe."

We got out on deck. We're surrounded by ice. I have the engineer go down into the engine room in a breathing pack and cut the power to the main deck because the grease fire had turned into an electrical fire. We get the fire hose and get the fire pump going. I'm not dressed for cold. I'm dressed just like this *[in a Hawaiian shirt, shorts, and sandals]*. So I decide I'll go into the house with the hose. It's still burning like a torch.

On my way in, one of the deckhands says, "Hit the TV with the hose. We need a new one."

I turned the hose on him and said, "You idiot—*we* own the insurance company! I'm not going to buy you a new one!" We're burning to the waterline in an ice pack, and all he can think of is a new TV!

When the water from the fire hose hit that hot stove, the steam almost cooked me alive. But we got it out. We had to float around for a while until the smoke dissipated, and then we went in and started rewiring, 'cause all the wiring had burned up. First we got the pumps wired back up so we had no free surface in the tank. Then we wired up the main engine, then we worked on the rest of the wiring. We got the bare minimum fixed and kept on fishing till the boat was full. We lived on cold food and on whatever we could cook on a couple electric skillets. God, that boat smelled awful for the rest of that trip.

"We all would have died."

—*Jake Harris*

My father, and grandfather, and I were jigging out of Sand Point, Washington, on our jigging boat, *Warrior*. It's 52 feet long. We were heading back in, coming around these rocks, and our main oil line busted, and we were dead in the water. There's a 15-foot swell pushing us right toward the rocks. My grandfather *[Grant Harris]* was 71 years old, bless his heart. He laid his arm right against the hot engine while he fixed the hose. My dad's up putting out a mayday, I'm sitting in the engine room, with hot oil all over me, holding the flash light. We're 50 feet from the rock face when my grandfather gets the line patched, dumps just enough oil in it to run the engine without it seizing up, and we got out of there. A couple more minutes of us being dead-ship, and we would have all died—three generations of us.

My grandpa acted like it never even happened. He never made a peep. But when he pulled his shirt down, there was his huge, raw burned spot where he didn't have any skin left. I said, "Grandpa, we've got to get you some medical attention." He never even went to the doctor. He just put some bag balm and iodine on it. He's still got a huge scar there.

"This sucks!"

—Josh Harris

[Fishing boats—whether catchers or processors—use a lot of power for pumps, hydraulics, navigation equipment, freezers, and the huge klieg lights that turn night into day when the boats fish round-the-clock. The electrical generators are powered by variations of the big diesel engines that run semitrucks—400- or 500-horsepower behemoths, with big, turbocharged air intakes. Several engines of that size may crowd into an engine room in the very bottom of the boat along with one or two really big machines: the boat's main engines that drive the propellers. Main engines are generally 12-cylinder, 1,200–2,000-plus horsepower diesels that can be up to 10 feet long, 5 to 6 feet wide, and 6 feet tall. These engines are so large, shipyard workers have to cut a room-size hole in a hull when it comes time to remove and replace them. Ashore, similar engines power locomotives.

All that power hammering away in a relatively small space generates a terrific racket—and lots of heat. Even in the Bering Sea, with temperatures below zero, engine room heat is often enough to keep most of the house of a crab boat warm. Inside the engine room, temperatures can be stifling. That's where the engineer and his oilers do their jobs when they're not on deck.]

We were on our way home, and I went down into the engine room to check the readings on the motors—the oil pressures, the engine temperatures, stuff like that. It's a routine check we'd do periodically. I'd just come off the deck, and it was 120 degrees down there. I tied my overalls around my waist so I didn't suffocate. I was wearing a T-shirt underneath. Well, I bent down under a generator intake to look at a gauge. The generator was going full tilt, the turbo was screaming and sucking in a huge stream of air. It sucked the T-shirt right off my back and into the intake and took me with it—right off my feet! My shoulder slammed against the intake opening, and there was this incredible suction. I was hanging in midair by my shoulder and I couldn't break free. I grabbed a pipe and pulled, but I wasn't going anywhere.

The suction was like nothing I've ever experienced. It literally felt like my skin was going to burst and all my guts were going to get sucked out through my shoulder. But all I could think was, "God, I'm going to break this million-dollar motor!" The engine was still running hard, but it was choking on me. There was exhaust coming out of bolts and places where it wasn't supposed to be coming out of. Up on deck they saw black smoke coming out of the stack and they knew something was way wrong. They ran down to the engine room. The engine was still running, and I was still getting sucked in. It took two guys—all of their strength—to pull me off. My shirt ripped and disappeared. The engine just ate it, burned it up. They never did find it. It was one long, scary moment.

I couldn't move my arm. But being the new guy I'm still worried about what I did to the motor. The guys said, "Screw the motor, you need to get up to the wheelhouse." It screwed up my shoulder but good. When we got to town, I went to the ER, and the doc said, "If you'd been on there eight to 12 seconds longer, it would have sucked your guts out." Half of me would have been inside that engine. They said it had happened before, and that I was very lucky to have survived.

This 16-cylinder main engine powers *Wizard* through the water. The dark round air intake at far right is similar to one that nearly swallowed Josh Harris whole.

"Pull a tooth . . . with pliers?"

—*Captain Phil Harris*

The day before we were leaving for king crab season, I had an abscessed tooth, and it was just driving me nuts. There's no dentist in Dutch Harbor, and at that time there wasn't even a doctor. There was an EMT. And he goes, "Hey look, I can't pull a tooth. I don't have the anesthesia, the equipment, the staff."

I said, "You got a pair of *pliers*? You gotta get the mother out of my mouth, man. It's just driving me nuts."

So I was sitting in a chair with two of the biggest guys on the boat holding me down. And this guy goes in with just a regular pair of hardware store pliers, and he's trying to pull my molar. And he ends up breaking it off. There's no novocaine, no drugs, no anything. I'm wide awake and sober. Now there's blood everywhere, and there's just a chunk of tooth sticking out, not enough for him to grab. We're in a pickle.

So now he gets a regular claw hammer and a chisel—a regular cold chisel you use to cut metal, not a surgical instrument by any means. What he hoped to do was get down to the gum line, and give it a real good whack, and hope the tooth broke in pieces that he could grab with a pair of needle-nose pliers.

I mean, that was about as painful as you can get. I've done a lot of things that were painful, and I can take pain with the best of them, but that was almost more than I could stand. There was blood pouring out of me. The guys on either side, they're puking—they're holding me, turning around, and throwing up on the floor, turning back, and holding me some more. I'm just to the point of passing out. And he's whacking me over and over. He pulled out a couple chunks, but there was a big bunch in there that he couldn't get out, so I went fishing like that.

After we made the first trip it was all I could take, so we made arrangements in Anchorage to fly a guy in—some sort of surgeon. The guy's name, I never will forget, was Luther Paine. They knocked me out, pulled everything out, and I was back on an airplane a day later. And in retrospect I should have done that in the first place.

"They go off like cannons."
—Captain Keith Colburn

Even just standing in the wrong place when boats are tied together can get you killed. The last thing you want to do is stand near or around a tie-up line, because you got a strain on those that is phenomenal. We broke eight of them one day. Big, heavy hawsers. They stretch, they snap, they go off like cannons.

One time our greenhorn decided that he wanted to flirt with one of the gals on the processor ship next to us. So he climbed up on one of these fenders, right next to where that tie-up line was surging, and

The Fisherman's Memorial in Seattle, the *Deadliest Catch* crab fleet's home port, honors the many fishermen from the area who are no longer among the living.

Working on a stack of crab pots lashed to a pitching deck, a crewman prepares them for launching.

was talking to this gal. I said, "Hey, knucklehead, get off that thing! Look at that line surging right behind you!"

Fifteen minutes later when nobody was looking, he jumped back up there to flirt with this girl again. Right there next to that tie-up line. It broke and lashed back at him, caught him right in the midsection. The impact almost killed him. He got medevaced out with a lacerated spleen.

"We saw stuff we weren't supposed to see."
—Captain Larry Hendricks

Once in the middle of a storm, we were seeking shelter. We were slowly making our way toward Shemya Island, the second-to-last island in the Aleutian chain and about 100 miles from Russian waters. We got close to the island, and suddenly everything goes haywire. We developed all kinds of electrical problems. Our radars went down, the radios got all staticky, none of the navigation instruments worked. It was like *Close Encounters*. We couldn't figure out what was happening, so we turn around, and suddenly everything's fine.

Then a voice comes on the radio telling us to leave the area. They won't identify themselves. It was a terrible evening, we were in a pass, the waves were coming at us from all angles, and all we wanted to do was get into some shelter. Then we saw a military aircraft come in for a landing on that island. I'm thinking, "What the hell?"

I call the Coast Guard to tell them I see a plane descending. They tell me to go to another radio channel. Then they say, "Just forget about what you saw."

Then I got it: We were someplace we weren't supposed to be, seeing some things we weren't supposed to see. Later we found out that this island was some kind of top-secret military listening post.

DESPERATE MEN

The physical challenge of crab fishing is staggering—and understandable. But as any crabber will tell you, the less-apparent mental challenges are far more intense: Constant danger, near-paralyzing fear, fatigue, and the strain of living and working with others in miserably close quarters can quickly break even the strongest of men—often with tragic consequences.

"He wasn't safe to have aboard."
—*Captain Corky Tilley*

There's plenty of drama in Dutch Harbor. Distraught crewmen get upset about something stupid, and they shoot somebody. I've never had that problem because almost all the boats I've been on I hired men I knew, guys I grew up with.

It's not very often that you fish with someone you don't know, and when you do, it can end up disastrous—like that greenhorn I had on the show who came up to the wheelhouse and said: "I'm gonna jump off. Tell the Coast Guard where I am."

I had to take him to town. He wasn't safe to have aboard. If you're going to jump off the boat into the Bering Sea when it's blowing 40 in 25-foot seas, you're suicidal. I didn't know what he was capable of. If he was suicidal he might have been homicidal.

"They get out there and freak out."
—*Captain Andy Hillstrand*

We've had guys quit in the middle of the ocean. You tell 'em to go back to their bunk and lie down. You try not to rile 'em up because you can't have a guy that's mad wandering around on the boat. Then you take 'em in as soon as you can, but it costs you a lot of money.

We've almost had to tie guys up before. They get out there and freak out. If someone did go psycho, we'd put 'em in lockdown for everybody's safety. But we've never had to do that. I mean you don't tell 'em something dramatic out on the water that's just going to make 'em mad. There have been cases where a guy has quit, and the crew gave him a really hard time, and the guy has just gone off. I mean you've got to sleep sometime. And if he puts a pipe wrench upside your head when you're fast asleep, there's not a lot you can do about it.

We're pretty lucky. A lot of guys used to hire just anybody. People who live in Alaska generally don't want to be messed with anyways. They go up there to get away from people and then they end up on a boat with a bunch of other guys. You can get a bunch of ding-a-lings. You hire a guy out of the bar, you're asking for trouble.

"What IS your problem?"

—Captain Phil Harris

I hired a guy one time for Josh's job: the greenhorn, the bait guy. And this guy was a perfect specimen of a man. He keeps telling me how tough he is: "I'm the toughest thing. I was the quarterback on the college football team. I married the cheerleader. I am tough." So I hired him.

We leave port, and it's blowing 50 to 60, which is nothing to us. And maybe 20- or 25-foot seas. Next thing I know is he's crawling up to the wheelhouse on his hands and knees and he's bawling. He's sobbing, "We're going to die. We're going to drown. You guys are crazy. You gotta get me off the boat."

This guy's bawling his head off, and he wants me to get the Coast Guard out there to pick him up. I just looked at him and said, "What *is* your problem?"

He can't see land and he just freaked out. These guys aren't so big and tough. They just think they are.

CHAPTER 3

LIFE AT SEA

Crab fishing in the Bering Sea *isn't just a job—once the boat leaves the dock, it's a round-the-clock ordeal. Deadliest Catch crews know that each trip is different—and that each could be their last. Every facet of existence on a crab boat is extreme: extreme weather, extreme exertion, extreme boredom, extreme terror, extreme camaraderie. Even—when the crew can arrange it or the stars happen to align—extreme fun.*

All of it is intense and absorbing, as Captain Phil Harris describes the role of a fishing boat skipper: "You have different scenarios running through your head constantly about what you're going to do and where you're going to do it—and other than that, the world doesn't exist. There is no world. The only world there is, is me and those guys on deck, and the boat, and the ocean. And that's it. The guys on the boat want me that way. They want me focused because they know that when I'm focused and on top of my game, they're going to be safe and make a lot of money."

In this chapter, Deadliest Catch *crews talk about what it's like to live, work, eat, and sleep on a crab boat.*

LIVING CONDITIONS

Never mind the weather, the danger of working on deck, the frigid cold, the high death rate—living conditions alone on a working crab boat are enough to break most people. You want to sleep? Change clothes? Take a shower? Eat regularly? Dream on! This environment redefines what it means to be comfortable and what it takes to endure hardships.

"It's all-out warfare."
—Captain Corky Tilley

It's all-out warfare. You sleep in your rain gear. When I worked on deck, you'd get what little sleep you could, wherever you could. When I started I'd sleep on the bait so I wouldn't have to take my gear off. I'd crash right on deck on some crab line and be totally content right there.

Nowadays they wear sweatshirts under their rain gear. When I worked on deck—before autocoilers *[machines that reel in the ropes, attached to the crab pots]*—I would have caught on fire, I would have been so hot, we were working so hard. I'd wear a T-shirt and a Big Mac flannel shirt under the gear, and that was it. You'd run out on deck, do push-ups on the rail to keep warm until you got to the first buoy. Once you started pulling the pots you were OK no matter how cold it was.

Your pants got so filthy and crusted with salt, they'd stand up by themselves. The only thing you change is your socks, because they get damp in your boots. If you don't change your socks, your feet are going to get cold and sore. They start turning white, and they get soft. I'd pack, back in the day, 20 pairs of socks, two pairs of Levis, a half-dozen shirts, and rain gear. After packing a big duffel my first season, I never packed like that ever again. You travel and fish with the least amount of clothes and gear. You've got to pack that stuff around everywhere and cross three or four boats to get to your boat.

Deadliest Catch producer Tim Pastore catches a few winks wedged into Sig
Hansen's bunk—camera and survival suit at the ready.

"You want your bunk."

—*Captain Sig Hansen*

You don't have a lot of clothes with you 'cause quarters are so tight.
You'd run out of underwear. You'd be making underwear out of your
Adidas training pants—lopping them off.

You get done with the day and if it's been a tough one, you
might grab a bite to eat and hit the bunk. You want your bunk.
You want to eat, too, but the bunk is the big one. You might still
have your sweatshirt on and it's all full of slime and jellyfish,
and your sweatpants are wet, and your socks smell like hell.
Everyone's done it. You just lay down in your bunk. You don't
put the sleeping bag or blanket on, you just crash. Or you pass
out on the galley floor in your insulated gear with the heater
on. The buzzer goes off, you wake up sweating from head to

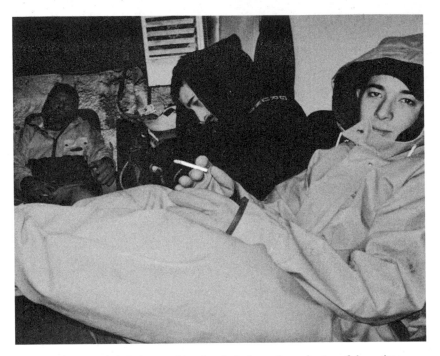

Jake Harris gets a brief, dry smoking break during a few minutes of downtime, rainsuit and gloves still on. That bleary-eyed look isn't from partying!

toe, and you go out there and freeze. It's no fun. Storms are when you can catch up on sleep. So there's times when guys are praying for bad weather.

"You wake up with fish guts on you."
—*Jake Harris*

Our bunks are the dirtiest. You only have so many pairs of clothes 'cause there's only so much space. And your living space is your working space. Our room is a bit ripe because Josh is the bait guy. It reeks. When that happens we know we better wash the clothes and take a shower.

But you can't use the washer in any weather—just at dock or in calm water. Otherwise it leaks water everywhere. When you can use it, everybody's fighting over it. You've got to be on top of your laundry.

After a month of fishing, the bloody things stand up by themselves. They're stiff as boards until you crawl back into 'em, warm 'em up, and your sweat loosens 'em up again.

We try to shower once a trip—usually it's a couple weeks before we even think about taking a shower. You eat your food, you fall into the rack, then someone's telling you we're a mile from the string. You wake up with fish guts on you from the last haul.

Cleanliness is not your first priority when you're fishing. By the end of the season, the boat looks like a bomb went off inside. On the way back into town, it's time to clean up. In the galley there's stuff slopped everywhere. On deck crab legs are everywhere, bait's everywhere. Inside you throw soap around and soak everything up. On deck you're knocking all the crab legs out from in between the deck boards, cleaning up the bait area. Around the bait area everything's caked with herring scales and eggs. It's like peanut butter that turns to concrete. Even a high-pressure washer has a tough time getting it off.

"Anything but this!"
—Captain Corky Tilley

When you've got those three- to four-day openers, I kind of laugh at those, because you ought to fish red crab for two months, then see how you hold up. A damn dirt farmer could make five days.

Two months on deck—it was ugly. I'd be out pulling gear telling myself I'd rather pack garbage, pick up pop cans—*anything* but this. This was too much. If you weren't making a thousand a day, you were pissed. The big money is what justifies it.

"Very painful."
—Captain Sig Hansen

When you're working for months on end on deck, when it's cold you get these layers of skin on your hands, they get so callused up.... I still have these hard calluses, and that's from 20 years ago. You'd wake up in the morning and stretch open your hands, and they would split open and bleed—it's very painful. At night you'd put bag-balm cream in a pair of gloves and wear the gloves while you slept just to keep your hands moist. Your hands were really abused back then because of the months of work. It was pretty tough. You got used to it though.

"I'll eat anything but a codfish."
—*Jake Harris*

Ever since I was little, they'd make me cook. I learned by trial and error. Sometimes the meal would look good, you'd sit down to eat, but after the first bite everyone just looked down at his plate. Nobody wanted to say nothing, but it tasted like crap. I wasn't much of a cook when I started.

Now I like cooking. You rock and roll. It's a messy kitchen when you're done, but it can be done. You cook periodically in stages all through the day. Next break you peel the potatoes, that kind of thing. You plan so by the end of the night, you have a half hour to get it done.

Eating's a challenge too. You get used to things rocking around. You get really professional in rough weather. You have one hand on your big coffee mug, one hand on your plate. Even so there's always something rolling off the table and hitting the floor. It's a mess, but you got to spill—it's part of being on a boat.

I drink a lot of water to keep hydrated. It gives you energy. I started drinking coffee these last couple years. Energy drinks—they help give you an extra little kick. I drink weight-gainer energy stuff, gallons of it. It doesn't work. *[He grins].* On a crab boat, working 18- or 20-hour shifts it's impossible to gain weight no matter what you eat.

Your body's burning all kinds of stuff. Guys say I have a tapeworm, that I'm eating for two. You're burning so much, you're always eating. You want to keep it full of fuel. I'll eat anything but a codfish; that's what we use for bait. We have cod pots, and we fish for our own bait as we go. Sometimes you barely have enough

Cornelia Marie crew Mark Anderson, Josh Harris, Jake Harris, and Captain Phil Harris down mess in the galley.

to bait the pots. Sometimes you have so much cod, you don't know what to do with it. But we still don't eat it. We eat halibut if it comes up in the pots. The cod are pretty nasty, especially when they get a little ripe and you start cutting into them. It's the *last* thing you want to see on your dinner plate!

"No one wants to cook."
—*Captain Sig Hansen*

If it's bad weather a lot of times we won't eat anyway. That's the time you just put on "storm soup." Take a big pot, fill it halfway, just eat it when you feel like it.

When I was younger the big deal about cooking was to try to get it done as fast as you can so that you're not off deck very long so you can help the other guys. So if you could cook breakfast in the time it would take you to haul four or five pots, you were a god. If you're hauling 10 pots an hour average, you've got a half hour or so to cook or maybe only 20 minutes. But that's having the table ready and everything ready to go. Well, I could do it, but it was lousy. But they ate it. No one wants to cook.

On the Norwegian boats with the old guys, the competition was to cook fast but cook good. My uncle was on for a few trips, and the food was unbelievable. He was just this old man, but he'd go off the deck for a few minutes and there was this five-course breakfast. I'd say, "How'd you *do* that?" It was all in the preparation, running in and out when you can. As you're working on deck, you run in, you may stir a little bit, you may get this going. You run out.

Then you've got your bad cooks. The guy that may take 15 pots to make a meal. No one's going to challenge him because, like I said, nobody wants to be the cook. He's out there for 10 or 15 pots. He may have thrown the bacon in the oven and been sitting there watching it burn while he's smoking and having his coffee.

"They're a bunch of girls!"
—Captain Andy Hillstrand

A lot of guys just eat microwave food. They're a bunch of girls! No one wants to cook, so everyone eats Hot Pockets. Well, we're brothers and friends, and we eat good. Neal cooks. We have chicken, steak, and mashed potatoes—John's favorite is cheeseburgers and chocolate shakes. It can be tough coming up with that kind of a meal on board, but Neal does a heck of a job.

"You get a feeling out on the ocean."
—Jake Harris

Working on my old man's boat, we enjoy big dinners when we're not hauling and the weather is good. Pot roast, ribs—we barbecue out on deck in the summer. Our bait freezer's huge, and our grocery bill is about 20 grand per season, so there's a lot of food to choose from. We blast the music, cook dinner, and everyone's in a good mood. You get a feeling out on the ocean—a peaceful feeling you don't get on land.

Bering Sea veteran Edgar Hansen knows that fatigue isn't something crews feel at the end of their shift—it's a constant condition once the season is underway.

FATIGUE

Working in extreme conditions day after day can turn men into zombies. On a crab boat 18 hours is a normal shift—and going without sleep for days at a stretch is not unusual. Strange things happen to bodies and minds deprived of sleep to that degree.

"I'm sleepwatching."

—*Captain Sig Hansen*

Sometimes you just can't wake up. One time I'm just dead-tired exhausted, it's my turn on watch, and the guy I'm supposed to relieve couldn't wake me up. He finally got me on my feet and literally pushed me up the wheelhouse stairs. He pushed me over to the chair and said, "Here; sit!"

So I'm responsible. I'm watching the radar, I'm making sure we're not going to run into anything. But I was dead asleep the whole time. My eyes were open, I remember watching the blips on the screen, but I'm sleepwatching. I was so tired, I didn't even know what boat I was on. I thought I was on the *North Command*. This went on for an hour. I'll never forget it. My eyes were open and I was straining to keep them open, knowing I'm on watch. I was half dreaming, half watching. But I did my job.

"He'd fallen asleep with his eyes open."
—*Captain Keith Colburn*

Once on our way into town I noticed the captain hadn't moved in about 20 minutes. His eyes were open, but I noticed they never blinked. I said, "Hey, are you *there*?" And he jumped! He'd fallen asleep with his eyes open.

"HEY! Your roast is on fire!"
—*Captain Sig Hansen*

I was the cook for a while, and it was hard to get up in the morning. One of the guys would poke his head in my bunk and yell, "HEY! Your roast is on *fire*!"

I'd fall out of the bunk, stagger over to the oven and open the door, and do "the drunk stand" and look around at 'em all laughing at me and say, "I don't *have* a damn roast in the oven!"

That's how they got you up. Whatever it took. If you want the engineer up and he won't wake up, you hit the alarm. He'll be up like a rocket. Hey—fun time!

"I'm hallucinating!"
—*Captain Keith Colburn*

You'd be amazed how long you can push yourself. You blow through your second wind, your 25th wind. One time I'm working on deck, we've been up for days and days. I got in this zone where I'm doing my job, but I'm hallucinating. I'm working on deck like a machine, but I'm back home and I'm 10 years old, playing in my yard with my brothers, and my father's talking to me. I think I'm actually there. Finally we blew a hydraulic hose and that snapped everybody out of it. We were all in our own little worlds.

"The whole boat fell asleep at the same instant."
—Captain Sig Hansen

One trip the whole boat fell asleep at the same instant. It was nice weather, we'd been hauling forever, and we finished a string and stopped for breakfast. We were out in the middle of nowhere, we just let the boat drift. Next thing you know we're all sitting around the breakfast table and we're just exhausted. Well, we're happy that we're doing so well, and the weather was nice. And then breakfast was done, and everybody has their smoke, and then all of a sudden everybody falls asleep at the table at the same time! I mean, I've got a mouth full of scrambled eggs and I'm *sleeping*.

So one guy wakes up and he sees all six of us sleeping. And he sneaks under the galley table and goes to bed. And the next guy wakes up and sneaks under and he goes to bed. Eventually half the crew goes to bed, and the other half is sleeping around the table. I'm sleeping with my face in my scrambled eggs and ketchup for six hours in the middle of a beautiful, sunny, flat calm day. We finally all woke up and just laughed our asses off. We thought it was just the funniest thing ever.

There's a 100-percent injury rate amoung Bering Sea crabbers. These mangled
fingers belong to deckhand John "Rambo" Mavar.

INJURIES

The injury rate for crab boat crew members in the Bering Sea is 100 percent. Everyone gets hurt—it's part of the job. And doctors and hospitals are hundreds of miles of stormy ocean away. Whether it's sewing up a gaping head wound with dental floss, working with a broken arm, or gluing a finger back together, crab boat medicine is not for the weak-hearted.

"We're not exactly plastic surgeons."
—Monte Colburn

One greenhorn, we'd probably told him 10 times: "Don't stand by the pot when we're unloading it. Get a tote under it to catch the crab and then step aside. If you don't, the door of the pot can fall on you."

Well, he was doing it properly about half the time. Suddenly he's right where he's not supposed to be. The pot comes up. One guy lets go of the door, and the door comes down and hits the greenhorn right above his eye. It was like an explosion—this guy had this three-prong cut that was an inch and a half in three directions. It was really nasty. And he was a good-looking 20-year-old kid too. So the chief [engineer] and I, we're looking at him going, "What do we do? We'd better put a stitch in it."

The kid says, "No way! I don't want *you* guys sewing on me!" And I don't really blame him.

So we took about 20 butterfly bandages and covered his whole face up. When we got to town, it took them about three hours to soak the scab and bandages off at the clinic in Dutch, but the doctor said that we'd closed the wound fairly well. The scar was within his eyebrow and down kind of on his nose. He didn't look too bad—considering we're not exactly plastic surgeons.

It almost seems like you get hurt more when it's nice out. When it's rough you're prepared. You're like a cat—you're tense. When it's nice you're kind of complacent. I don't want to say you get lazy, but you're just not as mentally sharp when it's nice.

"I thought it killed him."

—Captain Corky Tilley

I had one guy break his jaw. He was chain-binding pots in front of the
wheelhouse window, using a big cheater bar for leverage on the chain
binder. He was trying to pull the cheater bar off, but I could see he was
pulling it up too much, and the binder was going to release and snap
the lever. I was slapping on the pilothouse window, screaming at him,
trying to get his attention—but the handle snapped, and the cheater hit
him right in the face.

It broke his jaw, ripped his tongue loose—I thought it killed him.
He dropped to the pots like a dead man. We got him down. He was
conscious but he couldn't talk. I called emergency services at the
Ballard hospital and got a doctor on the line. We gave the guy a bunch
of pain meds and took him into town. That was one of the only injuries
I ever had. I've never had anyone killed or drowned.

"The guy on deck next to him heard it break."

—Captain Keith Colburn

On the *Wizard* I've been pretty fortunate. I've had lots of injuries
but nothing tremendously severe. About three years ago Tony—my
engineer and a good friend of mine—ran his arm right up into the horn
of the bottom of the block. The guy on deck next to him heard it break.
This was a seven-day season and we're 60 hours from town. So I had
him up to the wheelhouse and asked him, "What are we going to do?"

He's like, "Well, we're going to fish."

I'm going, "Are you sure about this?"

He's like, "Yeah!"

I go, "Do you need any painkillers?"

He goes, "No. I'll take Tylenol; if it gets worse I'll let you know."

Well, it got worse. I ended up giving him something, but a
painkiller doesn't do much when you're talking about a broken
bone. The splint we had in our medicine chest wasn't that great.
Tony, being the engineer, wanted to fabricate a better brace, and

we actually did. He had some round stock, some cardboard, all kinds of stuff, and put together a pretty good little brace for his arm so it was immobilized for the seven-day season. And you know what? We had a great season. He ended up having two screws and a plate put in. It was broken in two spots. The guy's tough as nails.

John, my ex-engineer years ago, fell off a 20-foot-tall stack of pots. He went cartwheeling down in front of me and landed on the deck a crumpled mess. He ended up compressing a disc or something. He's fortunate that's all that happened. He took two shifts off and went back to work. It's amazing what these guys can do and continue to work.

"Like somebody throwing a rock on your head."
—*Captain Sig Hansen*

The one incident where Edgar got his head split open, that was a piece of ice that had fallen from the mast. It wasn't that big, just a little chunk—but of course it's like somebody holding a rock two stories high and throwing it on your head. It split him open, and he's bleeding pretty bad, and we got him in the galley, and it was hard to stop the bleeding 'cause it's a head wound. So we got the pressure on it for a while, then we just had to shave his head a little bit so we could get to the wound and clean it out and sew him up. We just used dental floss—it was unscented, you know, so that worked. *[He laughs.]* So you sew a little bit, then use butterfly bandages, and then just patch him up and send him back to work.

Captain Phil Harris: Yeah, we've done that before. Dental floss works great.

Captain Larry Hendricks: The best thing that ever came along is superglue. You get a cut, you wipe the blood off, squeeze a bottle in there, tape it up, and get back to fishing.

Captain Phil Harris: My engineer cuts himself, and he's got a flap hanging out? We'll superglue it back together—and it holds great!

"Don't look!"
—*Captain Sig Hansen*

They're dealing with knives all the time, cutting up bait. One time Edgar was working with a knife in his hand when the line popped out of the coiler. Edgar grabbed the line with the same hand that held the knife and threw the line back in the coiler. But he stabbed the knife through his other arm in the process. The guys were smart enough to say, "Don't look! We'll take care of it."

They brought him into the galley, and he's sitting at the table and not looking at it. When I came down from the wheelhouse to see what was going on I looked at his arm I went, "Holy crap!" Which was a big mistake because now he turns white, starts sweating and almost faints. I don't think we had to stitch that one. I think we just butterflied him.

"A seagull started to make off with it."
—*Captain Larry Hendricks*

There was a guy named Arthur—now *there's* a character. He lopped his finger off in a power block, and a seagull swooped down and started to make off with it. Well, he got it back from the seagull somehow, but instead of putting it on ice, he put it on salt. He took it in to the doctor and wanted him to put it back on, but the doctor couldn't do anything with it. It was all dried up—salt-cured. So Arthur put it on a gold chain and wears it around his neck. To this day.

"Bones were sticking out."
—*Captain Phil Harris*

I cut one of my fingers off back when I was working on deck. It happened on the power block—I got my hand between a line and the block, and it just ripped the end of it off. The whole end was gone, and the nail was bent back, and some bones were sticking out. We were three days from town. The guys covered it up and saved the nail.

At that time there wasn't a doctor in Dutch Harbor, just an

EMT. He cut a piece of skin off the inside of my forearm and folded it around the finger, and put the nail back where it was supposed to go, and sewed it up. He said, "Look, this will get you to Seattle, but you're going to have that finger amputated from the knuckle up."

When I got to the hospital down here, the doctor looked at me and started laughing. He said, "You know, I'm not going to amputate your finger quite yet. There's plenty of time for that if we need to, but this doesn't look so bad. The sew job that he did—it is starting to *take*." They worked on it a bit, cleaned it up, but my finger is still there.

"That was no fun."

—*Lenny Lekanoff*

Once I had a pot fall on me and break my leg. That was *no* fun. It was just standing upright on the rail, and the crane was still hooked to it. I was getting ready to tie it in place when one of the pot ties I had draped around my shoulders fell off, and I turned around, and bent over, and picked it up. Just as I was beginning to straighten up, I heard somebody holler, "Look up!" But by then the pot was already falling. What happened was when he stacked the pot and swung the crane back, he didn't let enough slack out of the line, and the crane pulled it over on me.

It broke my lower left leg in two places. All I remember is just pitching onto the deck afterwards. The whole left side of my body was bruised up, my lower left leg was broken in two places, and it put a big hole in my lower leg muscle. There's still a big scar, and that was 20 years ago.

They thought it was a compound fracture because of the hole in the muscle. They secured me in my bunk the best they could. Twenty years ago you didn't have the best medical gear—no splints or anything like that—and very little training. It's not like that today. Fortunately we were only four hours out of the port of St. Paul, and they took me to the clinic, X-rayed it, put a temporary splint on it, and medevaced me out of there on a Learjet.

"I broke about everything but my neck."

—Captain Phil Harris

A couple of years ago I broke my back in two places. I was up on the boat lifting up a hose, and I hear this "snap!" I go back up in the chair and sit down and I couldn't get back out of it. I had to have the guys come up and help me out of there and get me to my room. Then I couldn't get out of bed. And I'm talking about some *serious* pain.

I lived with it for about a week and came home. A buddy of mine's a surgeon, so I stopped off to see him, and he gave me like 50 Percocet *[a strong pain medication]*. I ate them all in a couple of days. In the meantime my ex-wife is screaming at me about cutting this tree down, so I'm out with a broken back trying to cut down a huge tree.

Finally I went back to my buddy, who tells me to get an MRI. So I get out of the little tube they put you in, and the technician goes, "You're a crab fisherman?"

I said, "Yeah, why?"

He says, "Wow, you guys are amazing."

So I ask him what the problem is. He won't tell me. He says, "You have to talk to your doctor."

So I went up and I said: "Glen, what's the deal? Just write me a prescription for some really strong stuff." He looks at the report and says, "Phil, your back's broken in two places."

I said, "Well, why am I walking?"

And he says: "To tell you the honest-to-God truth, Phil, I don't *know* why. Ninety percent of people would be paralyzed."

I don't have time to take six months off for an operation, so they gave me cortisone injections, and it did help. But when I get out of bed, it takes me about a half hour to walk. I stumble around 'cause I've broke my back, one leg, all my toes, my fingers, my hands, my arm. I broke about everything but my neck, all on the boat.

EQUIPMENT FAILURE

The tremendous forces of towering waves, hurricane-force winds, bitter cold, and constant stress are as hard on a crab boat's equipment as they are on the crew. Just keeping the boat upright and running is a full-time job. And when something does go wrong, it's up to the crew to fix it fast—before it can disable the boat.

"Everything breaks on a boat."
—Josh Harris

Everything breaks on a boat. There isn't a product made that withstands the punishment of the ocean. Everything's being contorted, slammed, beat. Our boat looks great—because we maintain it. Nothing holds up out there. It's a constant game of "I wonder what's broken now—we better fix it." Most of the time the engineer does it, but we all band together to help out because as soon as we're done, we can go to sleep. You have to prioritize on how important the part is. It's a giant game of smoke and mirrors.

Equipment failure is constant. Whenever you have something that breaks, you try to manhandle it, strong-arm it. If you can't do that, you're screwed. You've got to go back to port and you lose a bunch of money. That's why you hire a good engineer. He should be able to Mickey Mouse anything back together. Otherwise you end up burning five or six grand worth of fuel just to get a 50-cent part replaced.

Jake Harris: The boat is your little city, your living space, your heat source, your power source. Maintenance is a 24-hour-a-day job. You've got to watch the fuel, change oil in the engines, make sure the pumps are running, check the refrigeration system—it's constant. On our boat there's a lot of space to work, but a lot of boats are crammed and there's not a lot of extra spare parts.

Josh Harris: We had a fluke *[a propeller blade]* snap right off one of our props. We had 'em worked on, and the guy who did it heated them up to bend them. Well, on this metal they're made out of, you're not supposed to do that. He should have worked it cold. Right after they went back on, we had a lot of vibration. We sent a diver down to look at 'em, and he says part of the propeller—one whole fluke—had snapped right off. He said we were lucky it didn't go up instead of down or it would have come right through the hull and sank us right there. The other prop was cracked and about to go. They had to blast them off the shafts with depth charges and put different ones on.

The spares, they're not right for the hull the way it is now. They were made before the boat was lengthened, so they vibrate real bad. The vibration caused a couple wires to arc, and they turned red hot. We were in Dutch at the fuel dock or we might never have noticed. Luckily we saw the power drain and ran for the engine room. Smoke was barreling out of the engine room door. We're yelling, "Fire! Fire!" We shut everything down and hosed her down with extinguishers for a little bit. A fire can sink you if you don't catch it fast.

We have to go out again with those same props. It takes a year to make a new one, so we have to go. We don't have a choice.

"When that happens, you're screwed."
—Captain Phil Harris

When you're on watch you always go down in the engine room once in a while looking around, plus we have all these cameras going. I have a great big flat-screen monitor and I have five cameras—one overlooking each engine in the engine room—that are always on. Every 15 seconds the screen goes to a different camera. So I can see everything that goes on down there. If there was a fire, I could see it. If there was flooding, I could see it.

Well, these last guys that sank, the guy on watch didn't go down in the engine room. The shaft runs through the boat, and on the end is the propeller. But there's an opening where the shaft goes through the

A boat is a marvelous collection of complex mechanical systems—all subject to failure, and many of which could scuttle the entire craft.

hold, and there's what they call packing in there, so the shaft can turn but no water will come in. But packing can fail. When that happens the water comes through that packing and fills up the lazarette [the rearmost compartment of the boat].

Farther forward in the boat there's another bulkhead where the shaft goes through to the engine room. Well, that packing's loose too. So water's started coming in on these guys, and nobody's elected to check the engine room. So the boat gets heavy. It's filling up with water, and nobody knows it. It goes up a wave and when it comes down it's so heavy that it just keeps going down. Another wave comes over the top of it and swamps the boat, and down they go. That fast.

This was in the middle of the night. And when they found the boat, it was sitting upright just perfectly, like it was tied to the dock. Only it's on the bottom of the ocean. What that tells us is that when it sank it didn't roll over, it just sank straight down. Probably within a minute. Those guys were in bed. When that happens you're screwed.

ICING

Ice on the Bering Sea takes two forms: sea spray that hits the cold steel of a crab boat and instantly freezes and sticks, weighing the boat down to the point where it sinks or rolls over. Or ice floes themselves: big chunks of ice floating on the water that can drag off gear—or crush a crab boat in its grip.

"We would have just kept going down."
—*Captain Sig Hansen*

Ice is the big enemy. I learned my lesson. I was about 28 years old, running a boat in the winter. It was blowing 45, but the fishing was fairly good. A lot of the guys went in to anchor up for this blow, but we just kept fishing. Next thing you know the boat's icing down. I wanted to fill her. I didn't want to stop to take the ice off the boat, use the hammers and all that. And I figured, "Aw, she's fine." So we just keep going.

By the third day we had accumulated so much ice around the bow and across the wheelhouse and on top that she was literally on her nose. All the spray sticks. All your windows are iced up. I couldn't really see the guys down there because of all the ice.

It was 3-feet-plus-deep on the hull. We iced up all the way around the wheelhouse and all the way up to where the railing is—quite high all the way up. Like a giant dish.

We took this one wave, it came up and engulfed the bow. I've got water up to my wheelhouse windows, and if you've seen the *Northwestern,* you know the windows are quite high. The boat is literally going down nose first. All I can think to do is hit full throttle and turn her over as hard as I can. *[To try to induce a roll that will spill the water out of the dish in the bow.]* I went to starboard. The guys were on deck fishing and they knew something funny was going on. They're hanging on. The next wave rolled us over enough that a lot of the water sloshed out of the dish in the bow and we came back up. That second wave

This ain't studio work: *Deadliest Catch* cameraman Zac McFarlane de-ices a camera aboard *Cornelia Marie*.

saved the boat. If it hadn't rolled us and spilled the water, we would have just kept going down. After that the guys chopped ice for 18 hours. I learned my lesson.

I don't like to push it to the limit. If you're icing your pots, sometimes you just have to just cut them off. You break the ice around where the knots are holding the pots, you cut the lines, and you just throw the pots overboard—buoys, lines, and all. You "suitcase" them, it's called. You just cut 'em free, trying to get that top layer off. You lose 'em.

A railing like that *[he holds up a thumb and forefinger, indicating a 2-inch diameter pipe railing]* may end up like this *[he holds his hands 3 feet apart]* after a day. You're trying to get through to the deck, trying to break off pieces. It's hard work. Grueling. You clear the ice and you go to bed exhausted. You wake up and break ice

Time Bandit starts to make ice during opilio crab season on the Bering Sea.

again. And then you go to work hauling pots. And then you break ice. It's hell. It's pure, living hell. Period.

When the ice pack *[many large pieces of ice floating on the sea]* is coming down, it can drag your pots five or 10 miles. Now you're looking for your pots. It's mass confusion. Everybody's gear is tangled up in everybody else's. Any crab that was in those pots is now dead because the pot got overturned and dragged on the bottom. If the ice pack pulls the pots off the *[continental]* shelf, they're gone for good. A pot costs $850 at least, with the line and the buoys. There've been years where I might lose 200 pots.

"A living, breathing organism."

—Captain Keith Colburn

Come February and March, seven out of 10 years you're going to have sea ice. It's a living, breathing organism the way it builds and subsides. You can fish right near the ice for a week, and it'll be 10 miles away. Then the tides get squirrelly, and here it comes. The ice can cut production to almost zero. We try to haul 18 to 25 pots an hour. In the ice it can take four hours to get one pot. You can add up how much lost income that is. I've found pots 35 miles from where I set 'em.

Playing the ice wars you may spend a third of your waking hours chipping ice. Usually when you're trying to get back to town and have a load of gear on, you can't get the ice off. A crab pot is a big sponge for ice. The bulwarks, the deck, the house, you can beat it off—but you want to start early. It takes five times as long to get through 8 inches of ice as it does to chip off 3 or 4 inches.

"I'm not going to risk my life for it."

—Captain Corky Tilley

I've always been really cautious with ice. I know the dangers of it. I've been by boats that have rolled over because of ice. I've seen the debris. If it's blowing 50 out of the north at 50 below, you don't stack a haystack of pots on the deck. That's just common sense. I like money as well as the next guy, but I'm not willing to risk my life for it.

"The best thing to do—sink the boat."

—Captain Larry Hendricks

Best thing to do when it starts icing, if you can, is drive up into the ice pack, *[partially]* sink the boat, and freeze yourself in. The more of the boat you can put underwater, the less there is above water to make ice. And in the ice pack the ice keeps the waves down. Fill the crab tanks and watch a movie. That way you don't get beat to death. Hell, we've got food for three months. It'll melt sometime.

"Spit, and it's frozen when it hits the wall."
—*Josh Harris*

It's always wild when you can take a leak and it evaporates before it hits the ground. Spit, and it's frozen when it hits the wall. It gets so cold, the top layer of your skin freezes and flakes off. The shirt inside your rain gear is frozen. Your fingers don't want to work, and you move really slow. When the crab come up, they turn into hockey pucks—their legs eject and they freeze to death right there.

If you hit a storm when it's that cold, you're going to make ice. Every ounce of water in the air turns to ice and sticks to the boat. It gets so thick, it starts turning colors on you. You got to slow down instead of buckin' into it and making spray. That's when you know how good your captain is, when he makes that decision.

Jake Harris: Ice makes everything a lot tougher. Normally you can turn a pot in three minutes. With ice it can take 25 minutes to get a pot in the water. Pulling up a buoy is a big project. Shots of line get iced up in the pot.

Josh Harris: Our boat will start to list, and then you know it's time to go relieve some of the weight. You can accumulate probably a couple hundred tons pretty quick. *Coastal Nomad* once came into port with 10 feet of ice all over it. No one has ever seen ice that thick on a boat. You couldn't even tell it was a boat—it looked like an iceberg. They had to chainsaw the ice off it. I don't know how they made it.

We use rubber sledges to knock the ice off. It's a pain. You got to get a good grip on those mothers, or they'll come back and hit you in the face. We've got a $50,000 paint job, so you try to beat on the boat gently to save the paint. We tarp the anchor so the ice will fall off it easy, but the rails and the hull, it sticks to them like concrete. It gets so thick, it turns a weird blue color.

Jake Harris: Ice keeps forming. You spend six hours clearing the deck and the bow, then go to work for 15 hours pulling pots—and the ice is back. It looks like you didn't do anything. It's a real tough way of living. It'll wear a guy out real fast.

Josh Harris: You break it, you shovel it off, and it comes right back.

Captain Larry Hendricks: Kenny was telling one guy how to use a pick to beat off ice, and the guy wasn't paying attention. You have to hit ice from the side or the pick'll bounce back off and hit you in the head. That's what happened to this guy. He knocked himself out. Well, there's ice all over the deck and he starts sliding over the side. Kenny grabs him before he falls off, and says: "*Now* are you gonna listen to me? Or would you rather go for a swim?!"

"They roll over, and everybody dies."
—*Captain Phil Harris*

One year it was really cold—about 10 degrees. Everybody's breaking ice. The season started the next day. We got our tank check, we were cleared to leave, but I thought, "Screw this. We're going to anchor up."

So I told the guys, and they're going ape: "What are we anchoring up for? The season starts tomorrow! Let's get out there!"

I said, "Hey, look! We're going to drop the anchor and we're going to leave about four in the morning. That way when we're traveling and we're making ice at least we'll have daylight and it will be a little bit warmer." And I dropped the anchor.

Well, the boat that had been docked up by me comes by—their guys and our guys had been talking all afternoon—honking their horn. They're leaving to go out and go fishing.

In the middle of the night they ice up, roll over, and everybody dies. A partner of mine on a boat I fish with finds a life raft. Inside there's three guys and they're dead. In the raft. Hypothermia.

HEAVY WEATHER

Violent storms are a fact of life on the Bering Sea. What makes them even worse is the sea itself. Shaped like a funnel, it channels tides into strong currents. It's also shallow, building higher and steeper waves than typical in the open ocean. When storm winds are blowing one way and the tides are running another, that's a recipe for a killer sea.

"You'd want to see it blow hard."
—Captain Corky Tilley

When I first got up there, it was an adventure. You'd *want* to see it blow hard. But once you've seen it, and done it, and worked in it, and survived it, you don't really appreciate it anymore. You don't want it to blow 100. I've fished in winds of 100 knots. We'd have to weld big shackles on the end of grapple hooks to get them to go through the wind and hit the buoy.

"We've seen some bad, bad, scary weather."
—Captain Sig Hansen

We've seen winds up to 130. That's bad. That time we heard mayday after mayday. A lot of boats sank. The Coast Guard couldn't keep up with it. That was horrifying. And we couldn't help. At 40- to 50-knot winds you can get around, but anything more than that … at 60-plus, you're pinned. When it's blowing that hard, half the time you're going in reverse. You're just trying to keep *[the bow]* pointed into the seas. You can't just stick it on automatic pilot, throw it into gear, and go up against the weather. When it's blowing 90, 100, 120, you have to maneuver. You can't use too much throttle because then you're gaining momentum and that's the last thing you want—because those waves are coming at you hard, and you're going to break windows and kill yourself. House-forward boats have been hit so hard that they've taken the wheelhouses and actually ripped them off the deck and smashed them back into a mast. So you've got to be careful. Yeah we've seen some bad, bad, scary weather.

Deadliest Catch cameraman Todd Stanley takes a horizontal shower while shooting in heavy spray.

"Look at the one that's coming!"

—Captain Keith Colburn

One time coming back into town, the waves were really big on our stern—real 40-footers, solid, one after another. We'd been taking a lot of freezing spray over the last few days, and since you can't see whether ice is building up on the stern from the wheelhouse, the captain told a couple of us to go check the stern for ice. Well, the stern is the last place you want to be in a following sea like that. It would be like standing on the bow when you're pounding into it. But we get on our rain gear and go take a look.

As we get near the stern—we're protected by the house—a big wall of green water comes flashing by us. I peeked around the house and all I could see were about six or seven of these mountain seas, one after another. So I turned to Billy, the guy that was with me, and I said, "You got to see this!" So I duck in and he looks and he says, "Holy hell!"

I say, "Yeah, pretty impressive, huh?"

And he says, "No, look at the one that's coming!" And all of a sudden you could see behind all the 40-footers a wave that's *dwarfing* the others! I can't even tell how big it is. So we ran back into the house and screamed to the captain that we had a huge wave coming. And he said, "They're *all* huge."

But then he looked at me and he saw the fear in my eyes and he looked behind us. He ran back over to the steering station and slammed the throttle full ahead to try to get some momentum to run with it and to steer so we were going straight down-wave.

Then we started to rise and rise and rise like an elevator that's going to go right through the roof. And as we got onto the crest of that thing, the entire 155 feet of *Wizard* was on the face of that wave. The top of it was a good 15 or 20 feet of frothing foam, and we seemed to hang there forever with the water just boiling away from the hull on both sides of the wheelhouse as we were literally surfing down the side of that wave. And then all of a sudden it went past us, and that was it.

"Our worst experience ever."

—Lenny Lekanoff

We were by the island of Amukta, and it was blowing 100-plus with 30-, 35-foot seas. Boats were calling in maydays all around us—and we're fishing in that weather, pulling pots. Suddenly a *huge* wave washed over the stern of the boat. We had 30 pots on the stern, and the huge wave knocked them all forward. They were flying *everywhere!* They could have killed us all—we would have either been buried in pots or swept over the side—but the skipper saw it coming and alerted us over the loud hailer to get out of the way.

When he hollers *"Run for it!"* everybody found something to climb. Nowhere on deck was safe, so we climbed the exhaust stacks, the mast, whatever we could. I was climbing over somebody's back to get off the deck when the skipper said, "Go!" I got up there really quick. I turned around and looked at other guys just barely diving and getting out of the way before they would have been crushed by the pots. I'm not kidding! Why couldn't they have cameras back on the boats in those days to record some of this stuff?

The whole stern was covered in water. The skipper's up there doing what he can, praying, hoping everybody survives. Then the water runs off the deck, and you come down and secure anything and everything you can because in 30-foot seas you don't want it banging and smashing around on deck, hurting or killing people or breaking things. Once we got the deck secured we quit fishing and just jogged the rest of the night away. That was probably our worst experience ever.

"Look out! Look out!"

—Captain Keith Colburn

Sometimes the seas aren't that big but they're really steep. Once we had about 15 pots on the forward part of the boat when seas started getting really sharp and burying the bow. Basically you're driving right into the sides of them. My friend Kurt was on deck up forward trying to tie a pot down when we dropped into a deeper trough than we expected. The next wave curled right over the bow.

I'm screaming, "Look out! Look out!" over the loud hailer, but it's too late. I couldn't see after that because all you see from the pilothouse at that point is spray. But Kurt swears the pot got picked up by the wave and flew right over him. I said, "OK, that's it, we're shutting down."

We shut down, the guys were just getting in the rain gear room, and we had about maybe 12 or 16 pots stacked up forward. I'm just barely idling into this weather. The seas are not that big, but they're just steep, and sharp, and they've got teeth—big, green teeth—and they keep sprouting up and coming over the bow. All of a sudden the boat drops into a trough, and I look up and this wave, I swear to God, it grew wings. It came a good 15 or 20 feet over the bow and slammed right down on the forward part of the 15 pots that were tied on deck. Each pot had two half-inch-thick pot ties on it. That's pretty stout stuff. It doesn't break easily. All those pots in the single block got hurled back from the forward deck all the way to the back deck.

And I could feel the boat get real heavy. As soon as the spray cleared, I looked down and all I could see was water. The boat was basically a submarine at that point, with probably a solid 5 feet of water on the entire deck. From bow to stern it's a 90-foot by 30-foot deck. I don't know how much water that is, but it's a *lot* of water!

I threw the boat into gear and tried to speed its momentum up—to literally drive it out from under the water. On the *Wizard* we have freeing ports on both sides of the deck—huge holes with valves on them that let water run off the deck but won't let it run back. I'm hoping those ports were enough to do the job. I throttled up trying to push the boat out from underneath it.

The entire crew scrambled up to the wheelhouse because they hadn't felt a wave hit the boat like that before. I was sitting there with the throttle pushed all the way forward, muttering, "All right, come on!" I was talking to the boat: "Come on, girl. Come on, girl. Get back out of it." Well, she did.

But the deck was chaos. The forward block of pots had been slammed 30 feet back into the aft stack. The sorting table got launched—we never saw it again. The coiler, which is bolted to the deck, got ripped off its mounts and torn off its hoses and ended up lodged in front of the wheelhouse. The big sodium lights were ripped off their mounts on the mast in front of the boat. They're 20 feet above the deck, which is another 10 to 25 feet above the water. Of the 15 pots maybe eight were salvageable. The rest had gotten smashed from 34 inches tall to about 8 inches tall—and they're made of 1-inch steel.

We had to get the deck clear. You can't have tons of unsecured stuff slamming around—it'll destroy the boat. So I told the crew to get out there and cut everything loose and dump it. It was like a surgical strike team—knives were flashing, zipping through lines, and all those mangled pots went good-bye.

Of course the cameramen wanted to go out on deck, too, but when you've got loose 700-pound objects flying around, the last thing you need is more bodies to babysit. You want guys out there who have eyes in the back of their head, who have been on a boat so long they can feel the waves coming at them, they can hear them, they can sense impending danger before it hits.

Even some of the kids coming up today don't get the experience because they haven't worked the long seasons. Yeah they can learn how to stuff a [bait] jug. Yeah they can learn how to close a [crab pot] door. Yeah they can learn how to throw the hook. But when you run into a situation like that—where the pots are all tangled up—they're completely baffled as to how to get that gear off.

SKIPPERING

*A crab boat captain is a rare breed—someone physically tough
enough to have survived punishing years on deck learning the ropes
and smart enough and driven enough to prove to a boat's owner
that he has what it takes to make a multimillion-dollar investment in
boat and gear pay off. At sea he runs the boat and the business, and
he's the point man for almost any decision of weight: from how to
manage the crew to how to handle a medical emergency to whether
to take a chance on the weather or ride it out at anchor. It's a big
job, one of never-ending life-and-death responsibility. Every captain
handles it differently, but all agree: It's the most complex, high-stress
occupation they can imagine.*

"You're everybody's mom, dad, brother, and sister."
—*Captain Phil Harris*

You're everybody's mom, dad, brother, and sister. Everybody has
wants and needs—and not only are you running this boat, but one
guy might be sick; he's got a really bad cold where he's really feeling
like dirt. Another guy needs a draw—he needs money sent home,
he's worried about his family. Another guy, his wife's going to have a
baby, so he wants to make sure that if the phone rings, we catch that.
Then the engineer might have some problems—the centrifuge *[a
high-tech machine that cleans the ship's fuel]* just took a dump and
one of the mains is leaking oil. So he's worried about that. We gotta
get these parts flown in—and you know, all this is going on before
we even start catching crab!

Now it's blowing 50 or 60 out. The gear's sitting in a spot where
there isn't any crab, so I gotta move it from *here* to over *there*.
And the weather's so bad, I gotta make two or three trips to move
it instead of one so I don't kill somebody *[by overloading the boat
with gear]*. To top it off, *I'm* in the middle of a divorce—so I've
got an ex-wife calling me up, telling me what a mother I am that I
didn't send her money.

Captain Sig's center of command becomes a center of attention during the filming of *Deadliest Catch*.

Then the processor calls up and says, "Gee, we're running early now; we're going to be ahead of schedule, so we need you back in to unload two days early." Well, *crap*. I haven't got crab on the boat yet and look at all the stuff I have to think about.

I've got like eight days to catch my quota. And if I miss that unloading date, I don't get another one for two weeks! They don't just let you run back in with a little bit of extra crab. So I gotta get the most I can get on the boat to get over there to make that date. And you know, that's a typical day.

"Your instinct is usually right."
—*Captain Sig Hansen*

You're part friend, part babysitter, part captain, part engineer, part therapist. Earlier in my career I'd say, "Hey, guys, what do you want to do?" I didn't want to make the call *[about where to fish or what weather to fish in]* and risk their earnings. Pretty soon you're going back and forth with your decision, wondering whether it's the right or wrong one 'cause you don't want to fail your crew. Eventually they say, "Don't talk to us. We don't care. Do what you think is right." So I knew after a while that these guys had faith in me. Just make your decision and go. Your instinct is usually right. They want that separation. I'm still one of the guys but they don't want in on those decisions. They've got enough to do.

We have a good system. There's a division of labor. Edgar pretty much runs the show down there on deck. There isn't really an animosity between Edgar, Norman, and me. Let's face it: Sig's got the skippering experience. Edgar's got even more experience on deck, and he's better at it. Norman's key role is running hydraulics. He's just super at it! Running the block is an art form. Running the block and the pick together is an art. Running the block and the pick and the dogs—and doing the launch at the same time—is an art.

Jake, our new guy, he's fantastic—a great guy. Super enthusiastic. Love him to death. But he's *overenthusiastic*. He's, "Let me do this" and "Let me do that." Even though it may look easy, it's an art form. You've got to walk before you run. The kid doesn't get that. But it's nice to see that kind of energy because—let's face it—our guys are starting to get older. Believe it or not, 35 to 40 is old in this business.

"I'm not going to coddle."

—Captain Phil Harris

I told my kids, "I'll give you an opportunity to make the money and that's all I'm giving you: the opportunity. You screw it up and you'll be fired just like the next guy. You know, I'm not going to coddle you along—you gotta stand on your own two feet."

And they have. I love those kids dearly but I'm not going to coddle.

And it makes their self-worth too, you know? They *did* this. This is an accomplishment that Dad didn't help them with. They *earned* it, they did it. And that's important to me. So when they get on the boat,

I relinquish them to the deck boss because I don't want them treated differently from the other guys.

But those kids, I love them both. They've turned out to be really good boys. They both wanted to prove a point to me—that they're tough—and they don't have to. I have the reputation of being a tough guy and dealing with a lot of pain. And they want to show me that they can do it too. They don't have to. They don't have to do that.

Jake is small, but he's tough. He can do amazing work because he wants it. Mentally he wants to do it. And it isn't easy. He's an amazing little kid. I'm certainly proud of him. He's earned my respect, and that is sometimes not the easiest thing to do.

Most kids growing up piss and moan about their parents, and that drives me nuts. They don't realize what they have. Family's a big deal, especially when you grow up without one. I think back about the hell I put my dad through over the years. How he dealt with me is beyond me. But he did. So I'm pretty lucky.

"I don't know how he does it."

—*Jake Harris*

My old man, he's an excellent boatman. I got to drive the boat a bit this season. He let me pull up on a couple of pots. It's hard, what with weather and the wind and the tide all pulling you different ways. It's an art to drive a boat.

The only times I've been hit by waves is when I was working for other guys. My dad's good about keeping the port sidewall into the waves so they're not coming over the deck and hitting us. He's a great skipper. He's actually not a yeller. He's pretty mellow to work for.

The wheelhouse, I try to stay out of there. You get up there sometimes and he's stressing out about this or that. It's quite the catbox up there. He's got to run the boat, navigate. … I can't even imagine the stress. It kind of freaks me out when he tells me I'm going to be driving the boat someday. I don't know how he does it—the amount of hours he can stay up and do his thing.

"So I just learned to lie to my dad."
—*Captain Sig Hansen*

Secrecy is a big part of fishing. You've got your little hot spot and you're all alone. You don't want to give it up. So you don't tell anyone or try not to. But even talking just to your partner boats, guys have radio scanners. They might be listening, recognize your voice, figure out where you are. So you use code.

I used to talk to my dad back in Seattle on the single-sideband radio. He had a radio in his office. And we'd talk in code. He'd ask me, "How many pounds of crab per day do you think you're getting?" So if I said "Alpha," it's 10,000; "Beta," 20,000. He only wants a rough idea. "Charlie," 30,000. "Delta," 40,000, and so on.

But then I found out that he would go down to the coffee shop and all the other owner-operator captains were down there and they'd get in a little group. Those reports were bragging rights for the old men. But then the other guys were radioing their boats and they're dialing in on me, and suddenly my little hot spot is overrun.

So I learned to just lie to my dad.

"If you don't know what you're doing, you're screwed."
—*Captain Phil Harris*

Through the years, me fishing on deck, I was on my ass daily 'cause the skipper didn't care. But *I* do care because I don't need somebody getting hurt. They're a family—all these guys. Not just my kids but everybody on that boat is *family*. They've been on there so long that I know them better than their wives know them. When you are so close to somebody for that long, you're not going to take a chance with his life. I've never had an accident—knock on wood.

People who think that they can beat Mother Nature—well, they're going to lose. Through the years most of the fatalities that happen out there are guys that take chances, and they've always pulled it off. They might have pulled it off for 20 years and they thought, "We've done this so many times it'll be OK." And it isn't OK.

These guys are smart guys—*very* intelligent guys. But there's so much that goes on in these boats—even the biggest and best in the fleet—and so much you have to pay attention to. You think, "These boats are indestructible. You can't sink these mothers. No way this thing would ever roll over and sink; it's just too big and too nice, too fancy, with all the latest and greatest equipment."

But it happens to the latest and greatest equipment. My boat out of all of them probably has the most high-tech stuff. But if you don't know what you're doing, you're screwed.

"Make sure that you're back in this boat."
—Captain Phil Harris

When you're in town you've gotta keep everybody out of the bars. They're grown men, so you just make it clear that if you're going out, you just make sure that you're back in this boat and able to work at 8 in the morning. Or else. Bad things will happen. Put the fear of God in them. I just don't put up with a lot of that. It's not fair to the rest of the guys. You pull that, you'll be off this boat. And they understand that because they're up there to make money. This isn't a social call. And I don't deal with it as a social call. There's lots of time to go out, but this isn't one of them. And usually they're pretty good.

We work twice as hard as the next guy to catch crab, because I have to. I don't feel I'm a good enough fisherman just to go out and hit 'em like a lot of these guys do, so I work harder than most of them. When the crew's absolutely dead tired and at the end of the day there's still 25 pots sitting out here; and I hauled them this morning and there's a couple of crab in them; but after hauling the rest of the gear it's way better over there than it is over here, I know that I'm going to move those pots before we go to sleep. I know that.

But I'll call 'em up to the wheelhouse and I'll say, "Hey, look. Here's the deal. We've got at least 25 pots over here. They're not catching crap. We can either sleep right now and get up in a few hours and then haul the pots over there or—and I know you're tired—we can go over and get them now, get them over here, and they're fishing while we sleep. Ninety-nine percent of the time they say, "Oh, let's go get those pots." But what that did is—that made them feel like they're part of the decision-making so they're not just "moving and storage."

You gotta worry about all that, but then you gotta worry about two weeks in front of you, what's going on two weeks from unloading dates, and how the crab are doing, how long's it going to take you to catch what you need.

It's a big job.

"People's lives are on the line."
—*Captain Phil Harris*

And then you got a film crew that's running around: "Now we wanna go up on the roof. Now we wanna stop and set this camera up. ..."

Well no, you're *not* gonna do it now. You can do it an hour from now 'cause we're going to be running this way or that way.

"No, we gotta do it now."

"*No*," I tell them, "we really don't. No, we're going to do it the way *I* want it done." People's lives are on the line.

The one thing I have to get over is letting guys do things the way they want to sometimes, even when I might have a better way.

When you're running a boat, you're in charge of everything that goes on. You're telling them what time they can eat, what time they can sleep, everything. It used to be that if I wanted a pile of wood moved I would not only tell them when to do it but I would monitor how they were doing it, and if they didn't do it the way I figured it should be done, I'd jump in there and tell them to do it my way. Well, you're dealing with grown men and egos. I have finally come to the conclusion that I don't give a flip how it gets over there as long as it's there. You know, a lot of things you just have to close a blind eye to.

"Most of the time you didn't know."

—*Captain Phil Harris*

In the old days all we had was RDF *[Radio Direction Finder, an early electronic navigation aid]*, which might give you a fix once or twice a day. But most of the time you didn't know where you were. We'd have to go out on the bow and sit there for hours looking for pots while the skipper drove around in circles. We might see one, and then he knew where he was. That was just doing it by the seat of your pants.

Then Loran C came along in 1979 or '80, and you could get a fix anytime you wanted to.

Now I have five 22-inch flat screens going along with three computers with big fishing programs that show you what's underneath you in 3-D, and I mean it's just remarkable. All the depths of the bottom are marked in different colors—you gotta learn how to use all that stuff. Sometimes it's a challenge. Sometimes it almost gives you too *much* information. And if you get too much information, it really screws you up.

Josh Harris: Everything's pretty high-tech up there. The old man definitely likes his instruments—radar, depth finders, TV cameras all over the boat. He's got more toys than anybody else in the fleet. He likes to be comfortable, to know what's going on at all times with everything.

"I get in my zone."

—*Captain Phil Harris*

You have to try to put tunnel vision on when you're running the boat. If I have outside distractions, you can see what's going to happen: Somebody's gonna get whacked. So I get into my zone, and they don't mess with me. I get so focused, I don't hear people talking. I can be taking a break for an hour and I'll go down and turn the TV on. If you came down and asked me what the show was about, I couldn't tell you. It's like you're in a deep trance, where you're only focused on catching crab and keeping everybody alive. You have different scenarios running through your head constantly about what you're going to do and where you're going to do it—and other than that, the world doesn't exist. There is no world. The only world there is me, and those guys on deck, and the boat, and the ocean. And that's it. The guys on the boat want me that way. They want me focused because they know that when I'm focused and on top of my game, they're going to be safe and make a lot of money.

Captain Keith Colburn: You've got all of this energy, and force, and noise. The hydraulics are screaming, the waves are pounding you, the engines are hammering away, but it almost becomes quiet. You start to put so much energy into driving the boat—focusing on the crew, the weather, the sea state—that you zone out everything you don't need to hear. It's exhausting. There are times I've literally crawled out of that chair. My legs were numb from the waist down. I couldn't even walk.

Monte Colburn: When you're outside there's really not a whole lot to think about. When the pot comes down the rail, you grab it and you haul it. When the skipper says dump it, you set it. There's not a whole lot to stress over. In the wheelhouse there's nothing *but* stress. These guys are counting on you. Where the pots hit the water is absolutely imperative. You've got to make that decision, and it can be kind of hard to swallow. You know it's like, "God, am I making the right call?" And then you got the weather to deal with. Nobody wants to run the boat when it's really crappy out. Guys would rather be outside.

PRANKS

Even on a cold and perilous crab boat, life isn't all work and no play. And when it comes to pranks and practical jokes, the ingenuity of crab fishermen knows no bounds. Whether it's to relieve the boredom, haze a greenhorn, amp up the friendly rivalry between boats, or just give the crew something to talk about as they go about their grueling work, pranks are the spice of Bering Sea life.

"Did you remember to feed the crab?"
—Captain Sig Hansen

Greenhorns, you prank them a little bit. If the guy has no idea what a boat's about and you're tied up to the dock and going into town to have a beer, you tell him, "Well, it's your turn now. You're on line watch." They'll sit there at the dock, you know, staring at the docking lines. But the boat's not going to go anywhere, of course. The rest of the crew comes back hours later and says, "What are you doing?!" He'll be indignant, you know, and tell 'em, "I'm on line watch." The rest of the guys will laugh so hard, they practically fall off the dock.

They've wrapped guys in tinfoil and had them up on the roof of the wheelhouse with their arms sticking out like a human antenna and made 'em move around "to adjust the radar." Anything for a laugh.

On deck you get them to feed the crab once in a while. You'll be working away and you'll suddenly turn to them and say, "Did you remember to feed the crab?" Then you tell him, "What? You *idiot*! All the crab in the tank are gonna die unless you feed them." So then he's out there frantically throwing boxes of bait into the tank. After a while you tell him, "No, the crab survive just fine on the nutrients in the seawater. You're just wasting bait."

What else? The mail buoy! After you're out there for a long time, you know, a guy might write a letter to his girlfriend. They got *me* on that one. You're writing love letters, and they say, "Well, you keep writing because we'll come to the mail buoy pretty soon." It was like there was this magical buoy out there, like a mailbox, floating in the middle of the Bering Sea, and a helicopter comes and picks up the mail. Pure fiction.

Captain Phil Harris: We actually had a guy standing on the bow looking for it once!

"They're screwing with you all the time."
—*Jake Harris*

Somebody'd pick me up and dunk me into a crab tank. I'd be soaking wet. I've been shot with pellet guns just to see me jump. I've had firecrackers go off when I was in the shower. Or they'd shut the water off when you're trying to take a shower. They're like big brothers, screwing with you all the time.

You learn a couple things and start firing back, but you never want to do anything serious to them because their trick book is a lot bigger than yours. I'm kind of a nice guy. I don't like to screw with a lot of people. But I've thrown water in their bunk. Or I'll hide something in their bunk—old tuna fish, some ripe bait, something you've been cooking that's gone bad—anything with a rank smell is good to hide in someone's bunk if you want a little laugh.

"The guy walked into his own booby trap."
—*Kenny Hendricks*

Sometimes stuff backfires. I was always the first one up in the morning. Larry would ring the bell, and I'd get up and boil water for coffee. He knew I'd get up—I was the engineer, and the engineer always gets up for the bell. It's ingrained.

Well, one morning a bunch of guys come back from the bar. I'm in bed—they think I'm asleep but I'm not. So they get this idea that they're going to squirt honey in front of the stove and get me in the morning—walking into the honey in my bare feet.

Brothers Jake and Josh Harris exemplify the kind of camaraderie that can develop among those who live and work together 24/7. Before they fished, they fought.

Well, that morning Larry rings the bell and I don't get up. I wake up but I don't *get* up. The guy who'd covered the floor in honey, he don't remember a thing. Finally he gets up and comes into the kitchen. He says, "Ha ha, Kenny, I got up before you today."

I say, "You sure did."

Pretty soon I hear, "Son of a … Who put honey on the floor?"

The guy'd walked into his own booby trap and he didn't even know it was him that done it! I got a good laugh out of that.

"A little surprise."
—Captain Sig Hansen

Someone will haul your gear and put a little surprise in it. I've seen toilets come up in pots, exercise bicycles, bags of trash. Or they'll take a thousand times more line than you need and tie it onto your buoy so that you're pulling, and pulling, and pulling—and nothing's coming up. It happens a lot when you're in a small area with a lot of boats in it. You're just trying to break the monotony.

On deck a lot of times you'd prank your fellow fishermen: pin the tail on the greenhorn, that kind of thing.

"One of the dirtiest tricks I ever did."
—Captain Corky Tilley

Normally it was all business—serious business. We'd fool around a little bit. We'd put things in some of the guys' boots—crack an egg in there or something. But one of the dirtiest tricks I ever did was at the end of a crab season. We'd flip a coin to see who got to pull the last pot. Well, I had pulled all season but I lost the toss. This other guy was going to get to pull the last pot, and I was pissed. I wanted to pull it. So I cut his grapple line 10 feet down from the hook and coiled it all up nice. When he threw it, the end of the line went right out through his hands. Meanwhile I was on the other side of the launcher with another grapple and I pulled in the last pot. He was not happy, but we weren't going to set it and pull it again.

"He looked like a mummy."
—*Captain Sig Hansen*
A guy was in his bunk one time dead asleep, and we took all the canned goods out from underneath the benches in the galley where we store them and we piled them on top of him. It was a mountain of cans. He looked like a mummy. Then we hit the general alarm. He wakes up but he can't move.

"A valuable lesson."
—*Captain Larry Hendricks*
I lost my whole season's wages the first season I was on a fishing boat. Eight hundred bucks. I played poker and lost it all. I learned a valuable lesson: I play poker really well now.

Kenny Hendricks: Nobody will play poker on *Sea Star* anymore. If Larry don't win, I win. We let 'em get careless. We had this guy— he'd made 18 grand in two weeks on the boat and he lost his whole paycheck to us playing poker. Larry, being the nice guy he is, charged him only half of what he lost. That was easy for him to do—I had 12 grand of the guy's money, and Larry only had six!

Sig Hansen: My uncle Carl said one time in the old days they were in the galley gambling, sitting around the old oil stove. Somebody made a whole bunch of money. The guy who was losing scooped it all up and threw it in the stove. He said, "If *I* don't make any money, *nobody's* going to make any money!" He burned it all up!

"He was completely lost."
—*Captain Sig Hansen*
One time we were fishing near the ice pack, and a friend of mine was drifting, so I tied up to him because the weather was so calm. I jumped on board and took his bearings—you know, the book that you write your numbers *[position coordinates]* down in. I hid that somewhere in

his wheelhouse and played with his plotter *[chart plotter, an electronic navigation instrument]* a little bit, so he was completely lost. Back then the Norwegian fleet was always on channel 12 on the radio, and you could hear him screaming in there, "What the hell?—I don't know where I'm at and I can't find my pots!"

I got on and said, "Really? Where's your bearings?"

He knew right away what happened. I let him suffer for a few hours, then I told him where his book was.

"One of Larry's favorite tricks."
—Kenny Hendricks

One of Larry's favorite tricks was to see who could get up the fastest when he rang the bell—only he'd tie your shoelaces together first. You'd hear the engine room alarm, you'd slam your shoes on, take one step, and fall on your face. Or you'd fall asleep at the table and he'd tie you to the table.

Captain Larry Hendricks: No, the best thing I did was that day with the clocks and watches. We were heading back into town, and the guys were all asleep. I knew they all took their watches off and hung 'em on a doorknob, so I set them all eight hours ahead. The ship's clock too. After four hours I got 'em all up. They thought they'd been sleeping for 12 hours. It was the middle of summer, and it was light all the time that far north, so the light always looked the same. The cook made 'em dinner, and when we got to town, they all got gussied up to go into the bar. When they got there, no one was there. That's when they found out it was noon, not 8 o'clock at night, like their watches said. They were mad as hell!

FUN TIMES

Pranks aside, crab fishing can be fun—either because of imported recreation, such as music, movies, and video games, or the simpler joys of being out on the water in a beautiful part of the world on an all-too-rare nice day, pulling money out of the ocean by the potful. It's a time to relax and recover between bouts with the sea.

"A guy would go nuts."
—*Jake Harris*

My dad *loves* the stereo. Up in the wheelhouse the first thing he'll say if you come on his boat is, "Check out my stereo." He blasts Journey, NSX, some awful thing.

We have some pretty nice outdoor speakers on deck too. He lets us put some money into things like that to help keep us awake while we're working. Inside we've got our Xbox, and Josh and I play fighting games. The old man will even sit down and try to play a game sometimes. It's pretty funny. Things like that make your stay enjoyable.

This season we're getting two flat-screens, one for each bunk. That way we can play Xbox or videos on long runs. We play boxing games, football games—two-player games you can compete with. We gamble on them, a hundred bucks a game. Throughout a whole crab season you can end up owing a *lot* of money. I've come into town owing 700 bucks to various guys, betting on this and that. And they *will* take your money.

Gambling's a big thing on the boat. We put money towards everything. We never get to watch sports, but everyone picks out their teams and puts some money down, and when we get into port we find out what happened. We also bet on little stuff—we'll say, "Oh, I bet you 20 bucks that this or that happens." It's kind of fun—relieves the boredom. A guy would go nuts otherwise.

The teamwork of deck hands, straining against the challenge of nature, is part of the excitement and appeal to veteran fishermen, says Captain Sig Hansen.

"Fishing is a blast!"
—*Captain Sig Hansen*

If you've got the right crew, the right recipe on that deck—man, fishing is a blast! It's so fun. It's the *most* fun. You can be out there all day long, and if the sun's shining, and the fishing's good, and everybody's clicking, all the stars are lined up. It's just like a football team winning a game.

I think the most fun I've had has been when I worked on deck. I didn't have that weight of responsibility that I do now. We had a blast.

"We decided to have an egg fight."
—*Captain Larry Hendricks*

We did a lot of crazy stuff. One time Kenny and I had an egg
fight. We're bringing the boat back from Alaska and we're the
only two on the boat. It's a beautiful day, flat calm in the middle
of the ocean. We've got the boat on autopilot, and I'm cleaning
out the refrigerator. We've got six cases of eggs on board, 18
dozen per box. They're expired. You can't eat 'em. Well, we
decided to have an egg fight.

It turned into all-out guerrilla warfare. Inside the boat, out on
deck—we were climbing the mast and throwing them down at one
another. Altogether we threw 45 or 50 dozen eggs.

Well, we had so much fun, we wore ourselves out and decided to
wait until the next day to clean it up. All those eggs cooked themselves
onto the black paint on the deck. Man, it was a mess! It took us 10
hours to clean up a mess that took only two hours to make.

"You can't beat it!"
—*Captain Sig Hansen*

I remember one time when we were on strike for a couple of weeks in
St. Matthew's Island. We were all anchored up along this island—170
boats up there. We'd take a skiff and zip around from boat to boat.
We'd get all of our little buddies—all these 14, 15, 16-year-old
kids—zipping around in skiffs. We'd go beachcombing—it was a great
time. You can't beat it. It's beautiful. If you had your little skiff, you
could go anywhere. You were free. You could get to the island, you
could go fishing in the river. Nobody had any fishing poles. We'd take
strawberry cans and wrap dental floss around them. Then we would
take some smaller nails and put them on a grinder and make a fish
hook. Shave off a piece of crab line that's got the yellow nylon on it,
wrap it around the nail and you've got a lure. You could fish in the
lakes and rivers and come back with tons of trout. You could literally
pull them out of a river. It was a lot of fun.

CHAPTER 4

LIFE
ASHORE

Sooner or later the crab fleet heads *for town and ties up at the dock. Whether it's for a few days' respite in Dutch Harbor or a few months vacation between fishing seasons, the crew gets to climb over the rail and walk onto terra firma.*

Many crabbers describe life on land as "a completely different world," or "my other life." This distinction has sharpened recently as crews trade days filled with film crews for days filled with fans.

Still, fishermen will be fishermen. For many the high-risk, thrill-seeking, life-on-the-edge lifestyle doesn't stop at the high-water mark. There are cars, motorcycles, and endless other distractions, in addition to family and friends they see too seldom.

Here, Deadliest Catch *skippers and crews talk about everything from blowing off steam in the Elbow Room—the notorious Dutch Harbor bar—to finding their adrenaline fix ashore, to spending time with their families and fans.*

DUTCH HARBOR

*Dutch Harbor on Unalaska Island is the **Deadliest Catch** crab fleet's home port during fishing season. One of this country's westernmost outposts, Dutch has the feel of a frontier town. Fortunes are made here, and lives lost—just like in the Wild West more than a century ago. It's where crabbers go to offload their catches, take on supplies, and enjoy a little shore leave before the next trip out.*

"Blowing off steam."
—Captain Sig Hansen

I like it up there because it's a melting pot. I mean you get every nationality you can think of coming up to work in the canneries and on the boats. You've got guys from Chile, the Philippines, Mexicans, Samoans, Norwegians, Swedes—pick a race, pick a nationality. Plus the natives that are up there. All of a sudden they're all in one little tiny bar, and everybody's trying to blow off steam—which is great, you know, 'cause you gotta blow off some steam—and it gets pretty crazy. Guys could be fighting one day and buddies the next. Then you've got all the different fisheries represented, so you've got that animosity going on. Like maybe the crabbers came in with a big trip and they're struttin' their stuff. And maybe a long liner or a trawler didn't do as well. Then all of a sudden the draggers made more money and long liners were the bottom of the totem pole. Then our industry had a little slump, and now the long liners are making better money than us, so we're the bottom—the scum of the earth. There was a lot of animosity. And of course just blowing off steam. Lots of fights—lots—fights over nothing.

"It's going to be brutal."
—Captain Phil Harris

The Elbow Room is probably the toughest bar in the world. I remember one night up there, there was this one big Norwegian guy named Dogfin. He could pick up an 800-pound pot, stand it up, drag

Bering Sea crab fishing crews live it up during shore leave, as here in Akutan.

it back to the stern, and stack it all by himself. He didn't need a crane. This guy was just pure tough. And mean, you know? Just meaner than hell. Nobody messed with Dogfin.

One year I brought up a friend of mine named Steve to go to work on the boat as a cook. So we're in the Elbow Room. And Dogfin, he jumps up and he's going from table to table, just screaming, provoking a fight. If somebody wanted to take him on, he'd beat the crap out of him. He'd say stuff like, "Oh, you think you're tough crab fishermen? Well, I'm the toughest there is. You want to take me on?" You know, that kind of thing.

When he came to our table he wouldn't look at me because I'm a captain, and guys don't generally mess with the captain. But he looked at Steve. Steve had never been in Alaska, let alone the Elbow Room, and he's pretty well horrified. I mean he's a civilized man. Anyway Dogfin reaches down and grabs a shot glass and he takes a bite out of the glass and starts chewing it. He sets the remains of the glass down and he looks at Steve. Just stares at him. Doesn't say a word.

I say, "Well, Steve, you've got two choices here. If you just keep sitting there you're going to take a beating, and it's going to be brutal. If I were you I'd take a bite out of your shot glass."

Steve was looking at me like, "Are you kidding me?" The normal reaction. He's saying, "But— but— but—"

I tell him, "You ain't got time for 'buts,' bud. You'd better do something because in about one second you're going to get yourself damn near killed. And all five of us at this table ain't enough to take him on." Dogfin was that tough.

So Steve grabbed that shot glass, and he took a bite out of it. And Dogfin said, "You're all right. You're a tough guy. You deserve to be a crab fisherman." And off he went.

Meanwhile Steve's spitting glass onto the table.

"Watch the crazy fishermen."

—Lenny Lekanoff

When I was a kid growing up in Dutch Harbor, we lived like a block away from the Elbow Room. Back then in the '70s anything could happen in there. Anybody would beat up anybody.

I never got involved in any of that. But as a kid I'd watch it. From our dining room window you could see people going in and out the door. My brothers and sisters and I would sit there on Fridays and Saturdays to watch the crazy fishermen fight.

You'd see the door come flying open, and somebody would literally be tossed out, airborne, with somebody chasing after him. He'd jump on top of the guy, pummel him, beat him, and we'd just sit and watch. When you're that young and dumb, you enjoy it—it was exciting. Remember we had no TV, no movie theaters—the picture window was it. And it worked! We'd sit there for hours.

"A lot of guys have fallen between the boats and died."
—*Captain Sig Hansen*

It's the taxi rides home that are bad. You're just trying to get in the cab before it's too late. The taxis are trying to figure out where you're going, and you don't know who you're sitting next to and what kind of a night he's had. That can get ugly. So you can survive the night in town and still not be safe in the cab.

And if you survive the taxi ride, getting back on board can be deadly. We had a rule that if you had to cross three or four boats to get on your boat, the cab would wait for us. I was very specific about that. When we got to our boat, we'd flick the lights in the wheelhouse to let them know that we got on safe. So many deaths occur from just popping over the boats into the water after going into town. Or maybe there was a party on one of the boats, and a guy wants to get back to his boat; now he's climbing over railings. They could be slippery, icy, or maybe there's a little bit of hydraulic oil on the deck. Plus you're climbing over stacks of pots. A lot of guys have fallen between the boats and died that way.

LIVING ON THE EDGE

As Captain Andy Hillstrand says, "It's pretty tough to beat the adrenaline rush of crab fishing." But crab fishermen never stop trying, even when they're ashore. Extreme sports, fast rides, and near-death experiences seem to be more than hobbies with these guys—they're a way of life.

"A pretty fast little car."
—*Captain Larry Hendricks*

Kenny and I were in a hurry to get home one night. We had a bet who could get there first. Kenny was driving a Porsche 911. I had a Fiat Spyder, a pretty fast little car. Well, Kenny's been gone for eight months, and while he was away they put all these roundabouts—these traffic islands—in the middle of his street. He piles the Porsche on top of the first one he came to. He gets out of the car and says, "That mother wasn't there eight months ago."

Kenny Hendricks: I'd like to have that back—not the Porsche, the money I spent for it! Not one of our dads didn't tell us to save our money, but when you're young. … Hell, I used to drive a Lincoln and a Porsche. Now I have a wife, a house, two kids, and two minivans. The money's pretty good, but it's irregular. We live paycheck to paycheck, just like everybody else.

"A bonfire in the back seat."
—*Kenny Hendricks*

When we were young we were into figure-8 racing, car racing. We'd get a '52 Chevy for 50 bucks and take it to the figure-8 races that weekend. We'd buy a different car every week and we'd drive it until we raced it and wrecked it.

One weekend a bunch of us pile in to go up to Snoqualmie and go skiing. On the way back the heater quits. So we pull off the road, yank the back seat out and put it on the side of the road, and drive the rest of the way to Seattle with a bonfire in the back seat.

"I shot straight up in the air."
—*Captain Corky Tilley*

When I was in high school, a friend of mine found a huge parachute washed up on the beach. So he says, "Great! Let's go parasailing!"

We cut a bunch of holes into the chute to turn it into a parasail. We rigged up a harness for it, put a big shot of line on it, put a length of chain on the bumper of his pickup, and headed for the beach.

I was the first one up. There was a moderate breeze on the beach, so he towed me a little way, and I rode gently up in the air. It was nice.

But as soon as I cleared the top of the dune, I got into the wind. I mean it was blowing. I shot straight up in the air 100 feet—that was the length of line we had on there. I was right straight up over the truck. Well, after I got up there, there was too much wind for the chute. It started flapping and diving violently down. Just like a kite when it gets too windy, it would swoop down on one side toward the ground and then shoot up and swoop down on the other side. I'm scared to death I'm gonna power-dive into the sand headfirst.

So I'm motioning to my friend—get me down! But the chute's pulling so hard, it pulled the whole back end of the truck off the ground and was dragging it backward over the sand. Before he could do anything, the shackle at the truck end of the line snapped. The line was stretched so tight, it shot back 100 feet like a rubber band, with the broken shackle at the end of it, and knocked me back into the parachute.

Well, the chute collapses, and I'm free-falling 100 feet towards the ground. I *knew* I was going to die. I was sure of it. I couldn't breathe, I was so scared. Like I'd just jumped into supercold water. You know—uh! uh!—you're trying to breathe in and you can't.

Just before I hit the ground, the parachute—BANG!—snapped open and let me down light as a feather.

We took that parachute right to the dump right then.

"No sane man would."

—Captain Larry Hendricks

I had an Olds 98 sedan once but I wanted a convertible. It was in great shape, a nice car. Well, I borrowed a *[metal-cutting]* torch and cut the top off. I duct-taped over between the back seat and the trunk, and it looked great. No one ever looked at it close enough to know it wasn't supposed to be that way. The car drove perfect too. The only problem was when it rained. My cousin came in one time, yelling for me to put the top up in my car. I just grabbed a drill and drilled holes in the floor to let the water out. I liked the car a lot that way, but no sane man would ever do something like that.

"Like holding on to a buckboard."

—Captain Phil Harris

I have a couple of motorcycles, and this last one I bought I really enjoy
a lot. It's impractical. Inexpensive it isn't; it cost $60,000. But every
guy in the world that has a motorcycle wants one of these. It's called a
Titan, and it's one bad-ass motorcycle. It's got a great big engine, and
it's full of horsepower. It's like holding on to a buckboard. But it's a
work of art. Custom paint job, everything handmade.

"You go 'WOW!' every time."

—Captain John Hillstrand

I have a Harley Fat Boy with nitro. I like to max things out. I like
horsepower, skydiving—I'm trying to get into base jumping. Stuff like
that, it rushes you out. Gotta chase that rush. It makes you forget about
all the little stuff.

It never gets old. I guarantee you, you do 130 on a Harley with just
regular glasses on and you go "WOW!" every time. You jump out of
an airplane, you go "WOW!" every time.

"You're looking for fun."

—Captain Andy Hillstrand

You have to be an A-type personality to really make it in crab fishing.
Not that you're all going to do crazy stuff, but you're looking for fun.
Riding horses at full speed, for instance. I barrel race, and a horse can
go from zero to 40 miles an hour in a couple of seconds. It almost
feels like you're flying. It's awesome. But it's pretty tough to beat the
adrenaline rush of crab fishing.

HOME LIFE

Sooner or later the crews come home. And when they do, it's not always easy. There's a big adjustment to be made, and some make it better than others.

"You have to tone it down."
—Captain Sig Hansen

Coming home can be a big adjustment. Especially with two little girls in the house. You have to be careful, you know? I'm not exactly the cleanest around the edges. You've got to think before you speak, and a lot of times I'll slip and I think I'm talking to my crew, and yeah we use a lot of foul language at times. It's like this Jekyll-and-Hyde thing. At sea we're very, very direct. There is absolutely no concern about anybody's feelings on the boat. Period. We don't care. So now all of a sudden you're Daddy. You've gotta be very careful.

I still like to go out and go dancing and have fun and stuff, but Seattle is not Dutch Harbor, and you have to tone it down. You can't completely take the fisherman out of your personality. You can run, but you can't hide.

"Night and day mean nothing to us."
—Captain Larry Hendricks

To come home and adapt to the working world is pretty difficult. We were raised to work—to work hard, live hard, play hard. Our work schedule is: "Why quit? Let's get it done!" When we're working in Dutch on the boat, we work all day, get something to eat, go back to work. Fall into bed, sleep four or five hours, and get up and keep going. On land it drives you nuts that you want to accomplish something and you can't do anything till the next day because someplace is closed and won't be open till tomorrow. In the Arctic half the time it's dark all the time. Night and day mean nothing to us.

THE SHOW

No one is more surprised by the popularity of Deadliest Catch than the fishermen. It's changed their lives—and their perspective on what they do. Here a few of them muse about what it's like and what it all means—and doesn't mean.

"The show is about more than just big waves."
—*Captain Sig Hansen*

When we first did the show, we thought we'd do it for one year. We thought that's all it would be and we're done.

The show is about more than just big waves. It's awareness. It's a little respect for what you do. Seattle is a fishing community if there ever was one, and you always had a lot of respect among your peers that were in the business. They all knew that hey—we're hard workers. But outside of that as soon as you said, "I'm a commercial fisherman" or "I'm a crabber," they just kind of looked down their noses at you. It always bothered me, even as a kid. In Japan fishermen are revered. The occupation is very respectable. Here it didn't seem like it for a long time.

There's a lot of guys—let's face it—that made a lot of money, came home and went ape, and did a lot of naughty things. They raced cars and were the bad boys. Fine—those are the cowboys. Great. It's a good life. But whether you were a cowboy or not, you got that reputation.

I remember my dad telling me one time that one of his friends had done real well over the years and he wanted to buy a house down in the Highlands. That's an exclusive neighborhood—the top. But even though he owned several boats, they said, "No, you're blue collar. You're not good enough." As a child hearing this you think, "OK, I'll always be here." And that's fine. But even if I'm down here, at least I should get a little credit for what I do.

Today because of the show you meet somebody on the street and you'll get this admiration and respect. It's kind of nice.

"We've created a workingman's cult."

—Captain Larry Hendricks

The most amazing thing to me is the world recognition—the astounding idea that people know you by your first name, no matter where you go: China, Australia, Indonesia …

We're just as astounded as everyone else that people are so interested in what we to. To us it's normal. People say, "How the hell can you guys live a life like that?" They think we're absolutely crazy and nuts. But we're just normal workingmen is all we are. We were just raised in this occupation where we don't know any better. Nothing fazes us.

I think *After the Catch [a Discovery Channel one-time program that showcased the fishermen telling stories around a barroom table]* showed everyone that we were just normal guys, that this just happens to be the way we make our living. And yet that didn't diminish people's interest—it increased it. I think we've created a workingman's cult: It's OK to be blue collar.

"The work ethic really shines through."

—Captain Sig Hansen

One guy who watched the show came up to me at the Boston Seafood show when we spoke there. He was standing in line to get an autograph from my brother Edgar and me, and he was literally in tears.

It turns out his 14-year-old son was just a pain: want, want, want. But he watched the show and loved it. Then he found out through our website that I was working on deck when I was 14. Suddenly I guess that kid did a 180. He's like: "I want to work. I'll mow lawns, I'll do whatever."

He wanted to be like Captain Sig. Earn his way. At Christmas he wouldn't accept money from his family. He was going to earn the money to buy his siblings presents—all because of that show and emulating me.

That felt pretty good to hear. So I think the work ethic really shines through.

You see all the easy ways to live nowadays. I have it different because of my grandfather and my dad. During the war they didn't have any food and all that stuff. You grow up hearing those horror stories and you know that you had it good. There's a greater appreciation for it.

We had it good growing up, but I never took it for granted as a kid. My father and grandfather—all of that community—they were pretty tough characters. They still had that work ethic. And that feeling that "you earn your keep" goes a long way. I mean, some guys, you know, cry 'cause they've got to put in an hour overtime. Well, shut up and do it! That's what it takes. I can understand if they're not into their jobs. That's different. We love our work. But even so, there's time when you hate it so much that you're asking yourself, "What am I doing here?" But we still do it. We don't bitch about it.

"Do I know you from somewhere?"

—Captain Larry Hendricks

No matter where I am, people come up to me. A lot of times they don't know where they've seen me before. They'll say, "Do I know you from somewhere? Haven't I met you in Indiana? Where do you work?" They're sure they know me somehow. They just don't know how.

Or I'll go into a bar in someplace I've never been before, and the bartender will do a double-take when he sees me and says, "I haven't seen you in here for a while!"

People want to buy you drinks all the time. The kids on the show haven't figured it out yet. They'll say, "Well, I gotta drink this drink— the guy bought it for me." If one of us older guys tried to drink every drink we were offered, we'd be sick for two days.

"Big TV Star"

—Lenny Lekanoff

My family and friends tease me. "Big TV star" is what they all call me. It's all fun in a way, but I'm the quiet, shy, bashful kind of stay-behind guy. That's how I've always been. Now I go places and people actually recognize me. I've had 7-, 8-year-old kids come running after me at the mall, hollering at the top of their lungs, "Are you Lenny from the *Wizard*?" People ask me, "How's your finger?" All the time! People I've never seen before. It still surprises me.

"I don't want to be one of those guys ..."
—*Captain Phil Harris*

People just want to meet you. They just want to touch you or have a kind word or be recognized by somebody that's on TV. So you sign an autograph, ask how they're doing, what's going on in their life, and it makes them feel special. That's my job as far as I'm concerned. I don't want to be one of those guys that when they see me on TV they go, "Yeah I met him. What a jerk!" I try to meet people just like I do everything else: I try to do the best job that I can.

"It's been fun."

—*Monte Colburn*

You go in a grocery store to get five or six items. It should take you six or seven minutes. And you run into somebody and you end up talking to him for 40 minutes. But people are interested and curious.

It's almost as much fun for someone who *knows* somebody on TV as it is to actually *be* that person. Because on the boat you wake up in the morning, you walk out of your stateroom, and the guy's got his camera 6 inches from your face. That gets a little old.

But other than that it's been fun. There's been a lot of times where someone looks at you like they almost know you. And they want to come up and say something, but they don't.

"None of this is real."
—*Captain Phil Harris*

I keep telling my kids—Josh especially, because he's really sucking this up—"You know, none of this is real. It's an illusion. If you take yourself too seriously here, you're in trouble."

I enjoy being on the show but I don't take myself seriously. I have a hard time with this whole thing of being somebody special. I'm just a fisherman. This whole thing is going to be over someday, and nobody will know my name. I understand that and I'm OK with it.

"It's the two old guys!"

—Kenny Hendricks

When we had the boat open to visitors up in Ketchikan, it was amazing how much women and kids actually knew about crab fishing—*from watching TV!* We were at the dock, and here come two old ladies, typical New Yorkers from the Bronx. I can hear them talking to one another when they see *Sea Star*. One of 'em says, "Hurry up, hurry up, it's the boat from *Deadliest Catch*!"

Then she sees me and Don [*Sea Star's engineer*] on deck and she says, "Oh my gawd, it's the two old guys—hurry up, hurry up!"

They must have been on the boat for a couple hours.

We met people from Singapore, Israel, guys from Scotland that fished the North Atlantic—*we* were quizzing *them*. It's amazing how many firemen and policemen say, "You guys are what we watch on Tuesday nights."

A couple of ladies said, "You guys are crazy." I told 'em, "To us, it's just a day at the office, like being a cop or a fireman—it's all part of the game." They started laughing—both their husbands were firemen!

Little kids, 8 or 9 years old, they come on board and they're telling you all about it: "The pots do this, they weigh this much, this handle probably runs the block, this runs the rack and the launcher. And the rules are, no greenhorns in this corner, right?"

I tell 'em, "You got it, buddy!"